Studies in Theatre and Performance

Volume 27 Number 2

Studies in Theatre and Performance is the official publication of the Standing Conference of University Drama Departments in the UK. It incorporates Studies in Theatre Production, which had been a leading forum for the analysis of theatrical practice, processes and performance for a decade.

The journal is now published three times a year. We encourage the submission of articles which are not only descriptive of practical research, but which delineate the ongoing analysis that formed a part of that research. Articles may also describe and analyse research undertaken into performance pedagogy. They are particularly welcome when all this is related to broader theoretical or professional issues.

The SCUDD Website Home Page is at: <http://scudd.org.uk>

Studies in Theatre and Performance is published three times per year by Intellect, PO Box 862, Bristol, BS99 1DE, UK. The current subscription rates are £30 (personal) and £210 (institutional). Postage is free within the UK. A postage charge of £5 is made for subscriptions within Europe and £10 for subscriptions outside of Europe. Enquiries and bookings for advertising should be addressed to: Journals Manager, Intellect, PO Box 862, Bristol, BS99 1DE, UK.

Editors
Peter Thomson
Dept. of Drama
University of Exeter
Thornlea
New North Road
Exeter
EX4 4LA
UK
+44 (0)1392 264580
p.w.thomson@exeter.ac.uk

Lesley Wade
Dept. of Drama
University of Exeter
+44 (0)1392 264587

Associate Editors
Anuradha Kapur
National School of Drama, India

Laurence Senelick
Tufts University, USA

Reviews Editor
Rebecca Loukes
Dept. of Drama
University of Exeter
+44 (0) 1392 262334
r.m.loukes@exeter.ac.uk

ISSN 1468–2761

Printed and bound in Great Britain by 4edge, UK

Editorial notes to contributors

Submissions

Manuscripts should be sent to the Editors, Studies in Theatre and Performance, Thornlea, New North Road, Exeter, Devon, EX4 4LA UK. Tel: +44 (0) 1392 264580; Fax: +44 (0) 1392 264594. Enquiries and communication should be sent by email where possible to: p.w.thomson@exeter.ac.uk

Articles can be considered if two copies of each manuscript and an e-mail attachment (addressed to P.W.Thomson@exeter.ac.uk) are submitted. Contributions should be typed on one side of the paper, double spaced and with ample margins. The title of the paper should be written in bold and followed by a list of about six key-words and a brief abstract (c. 100–150 words). Articles should not normally exceed 6000 words in length. It will be helpful if the author also submits brief notes on him/herself (affiliation, research interests etc.) on a separate sheet of paper. Each article submitted should conclude with a list of Works Cited. Articles accepted become the copyright of the journal unless otherwise specifically agreed.

Language

The journal uses standard British English, and the Editors reserve the right to alter usage to that end. Because of the interdisciplinary nature of the readership, jargon is to be avoided. Simple sentence structures are of great benefit to readers for whom English is a second language.

Illustrations

Illustrations are welcome. Generally only black & white is available. Photographs should be black and white glossy. All slides should be printed as colour photos or copied onto PhotoCD as a YCC computer file.

Line drawings, diagrams, etc. should be in a camera-ready state, capable of reduction, or as a Macintosh EPS or TIFF file with hard copy output.

All illustrations, photographs, diagrams, etc. should follow the same numerical sequence and be shown as Figure 1, Figure 2, etc. Indicate the source below. When they are on a separate sheet or file, indication must be given as to where they should be placed in the text.

We regret that illustrations submitted for publication cannot be returned.

Captions

All illustrations should be accompanied by a caption, which should include the Figure number and an acknowledgement to the holder of the copyright. The author has the responsibility to ensure that the proper permissions are obtained.

Notes

These should be kept to a minimum, and be identified by a superscript numeral in the text. Please do not format your notes, but type them in list form at the end.

Referees

Studies in Theatre and Performance is a refereed journal. Strict anonymity is accorded to both authors and referees.

Opinion

The views expressed in Studies in Theatre and Performance are those of the authors, and do not necessarily coincide with those of the Editors or the Editorial or Advisory Boards.

STP Online

Electronic articles may be sent to the editors for refereeing (L.A.Wade@exeter.ac.uk). They should be specifically designed for electronic production. Previous articles are available on the website: http://www.scudd.org/estp/index.html

Studies in Theatre and Performance Volume 27 Number 2 © 2007 Intellect Ltd
Article. English language. doi: 10.1386/stap.27.2.95/1

'Umuntu, Ngumuntu, Ngabantu': The story of the African choir

Jane Collins

Abstract

This article describes a collaborative practice-as-research project that is being developed by the Market Theatre Laboratory in Johannesburg and Wimbledon College of Art in the United Kingdom. The article seeks to explain some of the ways in which an analysis of the costumes and stage design of performances by a South African choir that toured Britain at the end of the nineteenth century are being used as a starting point for a new work for the stage. The project uses the medium of performance in order to investigate the production and reception of performance, under the colonial gaze, by a group of young, black South Africans. It offers a critical perspective on the way in which this group attempted to construct a 'stage' identity designed to meet the expectations of western audiences, and speculates about the extent to which the failure of the tour may be attributed to the Choir's failure to fulfil these expectations.

Keywords

identity
Africa
Victorian
colonial
costume
audience

Performing identities in Victorian Britain

Between 1891 and 1893 a group of young black South Africans toured England, Scotland and Ireland. They were a Christian choir apparently on a mission to raise funds for a technical school in Kimberley [Plate 1]. However, once in England, a more complex set of motives for the trip emerged. On the tour they struggled to come to terms with the realities of late Victorian industrial society, which challenged their notions of progress and made them question their own identity as the black educated elite. The tour failed to make money and as a result they were forced to take radical measures to attract larger audiences. It all ended in disaster with the choir abandoned by their managers and left penniless in a London hotel. One of their members was the young Charlotte Manye, who eventually went on to find the Bantu Women's League and became a prominent activist for women's rights in South Africa. Later in her life she also campaigned vehemently for women to be represented in the newly formed African National Congress. What happened to the Choir, their passage around the United Kingdom and eventually across to America, is well chronicled by Veit Erlmann in *Music Modernity and the Global Imagination*, in which he sets the experiences of this group of young people within the broader context of late 19th century spectacle and imperialist imaginings.

The intention of this article is not to replicate Erlmann's extensive research but to describe the ways in which it has been used as a springboard

Plate 1: The African Choir in Victorian dress (1891).

for a new work for the stage. This work, which is still in development, uses the medium of performance to speculate about the way the performances by this group of young black artists at the end of the nineteenth century might have been constructed for their predominantly white middle-class audience. In particular it attempts to understand the reasoning behind a decision that was taken at some point during the tour by these mission-educated, urbanised black South Africans to perform in 'native' dress for the first half of their concert. This decision contributed to their performance being dubbed in one newspaper review as 'Africa Civilised and Africa Uncivilised' (*Irish Times*, 15 March 1892) [Plate 2].

Erlmann proposes the notion of the 'co-authoring of global identities' as part and parcel of imperial practice. He argues that 'the African faith in Western fictions of modernity and progress was worked out through Western assumptions about Africans, as they were in turn enabled by African stagings of something taken for an African past' (Erlmann: 10).

This raises questions as to the extent to which the members of the Choir were complicit in this depiction of themselves. How much was this presentation of self due to the demands of the box-office and how much were they knowingly pandering to the desire of English audiences to have their preconceptions about Africa and the 'African' confirmed? The new work considers these questions in relation to nineteenth-century performance, but also, by implication, raises questions about the production and reception of current work from the continent of Africa and specifically the ways in which live performance is contributing to the construction of identity/identities in the relationships between South Africa and the West.

Jane Collins

Plate 2: 'Africa uncivilized'. Photo from The Review of Reviews, *September 1891.*

1. For more information on the Jubilee Singers, see Viet Erlmann, 'A feeling of prejudice: Orpheus M. McAdoo and the Virginia Jubilee Singers in South Africa, 1890–1898', *Journal of South African Studies* 14: 3 (April 1988), pp. 331–50.

2. Diamonds were discovered in the town of Kimberley in the late 1870s, and prospectors from all over the world flooded there. Consequently, by the 1890s, Kimberley was a rapidly expanding city. De Beers Consolidated Mines, owned by Cecil Rhodes, controlled the industry, which was sustained by cheap African labour.

3. Lovedale was the major missionary education centre in South Africa throughout the nineteenth century. Established in 1824, it initially pursued an 'assimilationist' policy creating an educated elite made up of a small minority of Africans. See Saayman W., 'Subversive subservience: Z.K. Matthews and missionary education in South Africa', www.geocities.com/ missionalia/saayman. htm

The Choir was recruited by two British promoters, Balmer and Letty, possibly inspired by the success of the Virginia Jubilee Singers, an African American Minstrel Troupe that toured South Africa in the 1890s led by the charismatic Orpheus McAdoo.[1] The balance between profit and philanthropy in the motivation of the promoters and the performers is difficult to judge at this distance. The Choir ostensibly wanted to raise money for a technical school in Kimberley,[2] to improve the lot of the black labour force who were being drawn in large numbers into the diamond mines, but this charitable tag was denounced by one of the Choir members on his return to South Africa as just a fine rolling phrase (Paul Xinwine, in South Africa, September 1892) [Plate 3].

Charlotte Manye certainly presented the tour as a fund-raising expedition when the choir arrived in London. In an interview with London journalist William Stead in September 1891, early in the tour, she said, 'Let us be in Africa even as you are in England . . . . Help us to found the schools for which we pray, where our people could learn to labour, to build; to acquire your skill with their hands' (*The Review of Reviews*, September 1891).

Charlotte and her younger sister Katie were living in Kimberley when they were recruited; other members of the Choir came from the progressive and liberal Lovedale Community College on the Eastern Cape,[3] and however mixed the motives for the expedition may have been their concerts certainly represented a new stage role for black performers, at odds with the standard practice described by Ben Shephard: 'By the late nineteenth century, the British had a long history of putting black people on the stage and had evolved stock roles for them to play. Blacks could be freaks, savages, angels, minstrels, slaves and warriors and were variously used to

4. Shephard discusses the *Savage South Africa Show* at Earl's Court, London 1899, a spectacular re-enactment of the Matabele Wars of the 1890s. He also charts the love affair between Peter Lobengula, one of the stars of the show who claimed to be the son of the Matabele King Lobengula, and a Cornish woman, Kitty Jewell.

Plate 3: Charlotte Manye, from the New African Movement website (http://www. pitzer.edu/New_African_Movement/newafrre/writers/maxeke.shtml).

instil fear, loathing, compassion, wonder or sexual delight' (Shephard: 57).[4] The Choir appeared to want to offer an alternative to these stereotypical representations; at least, that was how the *Christian Express*, a monthly periodical published in South Africa, framed the expedition: 'The choir was organised with the professed object of deepening and extending the widespread interest in Africa and the African and of endeavouring to show the capability of the South African native in a novel direction' (August 1892).

The group of fifteen arrived in England in the summer of 1891 and immediately embarked on an arduous touring schedule often playing one-night stands. They were initially very successful and a performance at London's Crystal Palace led to their being invited down to Osborne on the Isle of Wight to perform for Queen Victoria. Their repertoire seems to have changed as the tour progressed, but basically they performed a combination of traditional songs, Christian hymns and English ballads. They travelled north to the big industrial cities of England, continued into Scotland, which had strong links with South Africa through the missionary societies, and eventually went across to Ireland. By Christmas 1891, however, underlying divisions with the management and among the Choir themselves were beginning to surface. They had not been paid, or certainly had not been paid what they were promised, since leaving South Africa. The managers claimed this was because the expenses of touring outweighed the profits from the concerts, but Paul Xinwine, one of the senior members of the Choir, challenged this. Xinwine was a prominent intellectual and a successful businessman on the Cape who had invested his own money in the venture. Able and articulate, Xinwine expected to meet the English on equal terms and was furious when he was refused representation on the management committee of the choir. His belief that the managers may have been engaged in 'creative accounting' appears to have been well founded. He employed a solicitor, only to discover that English law was tailored to work for the English and that the Choir was bound by a contract that they could not get out of. On return to the Cape he wrote in the magazine *South Africa:*

> I advanced to them £30 or its equivalent of which they only paid me five. In the same way another member of the choir lent them £100 at Kimberley and goodness knows if he will ever recover it. They say they can show their books and accounts in order to prove that they have been losing money. It is a perfectly easy thing to put any figures in books! Why, you have false balance sheets with banks which are supposed to have strict and proper auditors how much easier for a body of men who are their own auditors.

Xinwine also continued to challenge the charitable status of the tour: 'The venture of the choir was a monetary speculation in spite of all the platform declarations' (*South Africa*, September 1892).

The 'platform declarations' were the appeals for funds at the end of each concert to help build the technical school in Kimberley. Xinwine challenged the manager's claims that this was the main motive behind the tour, and refuted Charlotte Manye's remarks in the interview with William Stead in the *Review of Reviews* by suggesting that her real motive was political. She had, he insisted, set out from the very beginning to try to persuade the English to take action against the encroaching power of the emerging settler class in South Africa and the ruthlessness of the Boers.

The tensions between Xinwine, the managers and Charlotte appear to have come to a head in Manchester in December 1891. Xinwine wanted to abandon the tour and return home, Charlotte wanted to continue, and went behind Xinwine's back to the managers claiming that the majority of the members wanted to stay. Xinwine was furious and, supported by his wife Eleanor who was also a choir member, accused Charlotte of splitting the loyalty of the group. Charlotte attacked Eleanor in the restaurant of the Trevelyan Hotel and was hauled up before Manchester Magistrates on a charge of assault. She pleaded guilty and was bound over to keep the peace for the sum of five pounds and ordered to pay costs. The Xinwines were dispatched back to South Africa, followed a few weeks later by two other members of the Choir.

Diminished in number the Choir soldiered on, but by the summer of 1892 the potentially 'comic' exchange of blows in the Manchester hotel had taken a tragic turn. Before his departure Xinwine had been accused by the managers of having an affair with Sannie Koofman, one of the younger members of the group. Xinwine vigorously denied the allegation, claiming it was put forward as a convenient excuse by the management to get rid of him. However, Sannie· Koofman had a stillborn baby boy in Chesterfield in June 1892, and when the tiny body was discovered hidden in a trunk she was charged and imprisoned by Chesterfield magistrates for 'concealment of birth'. Another choir member, a journalist called Josiah Semouse, kept a diary of the tour, but by the end of 1892 his entries dry up. It seems that the Choir limped on until early 1893, failing to make ends meet, until they were finally abandoned by the managers in a cheap London Hotel. Cold and disillusioned, they were eventually rescued by the charitable offices of the Missionary Society who raised the funds to send them home.

It is an extraordinary story situated somewhere between melodrama and the Victorian novel, but the relationships between the main protagonists and the desire to apportion 'blame' in the manner of those genres, is complicated by the fact that two years later Charlotte Manye and a small number of the original Choir set out on another expedition with Balmer and Letty, this time to America.

As a writer and researcher of performance my interest in the story lay in the dramatic potential of the difference between the private and public worlds of the tour; and the human cost to the individual choir members of perpetually being 'on show' as the 'exotic other'. This seems to have been compounded by the decision of the Choir, early in the tour, to fashion themselves in the 'role' of pre-christianised heathen for the first half of the concert, a decision that, judging by the correspondence between London and the Cape around this issue of sartorial representation, would not have been made without a lot of soul-searching. Underpinning all the above was the wish to exploit the potential of the medium of performance to explore the 'colonial gaze', thus anticipating Erlmann's proposition concerning the 'co-authoring of global identities.'

Whatever the credibility of Paul Xinwine's reservations about her motives, Charlotte Manye's plea for funds in the *Review of Reviews* was timely. It re-asserted the value of education and progress at precisely the point when confidence and belief in the humanitarian and philanthropic purposes of the 'civilizing' mission of Empire were fading among certain sectors of the educated Victorian middle classes. The evidence of blatant exploitation and materialism in the scramble for gold and diamonds on the Cape, coupled with a waning of belief in the concept of 'progress', was undermining the certainties of the earlier part of the century.[5] If the audience was looking for re-assurance of the centrality of its position in the global world-order and a justification for colonial expansion, then Charlotte's speech provided it. The reader and potential audience sees itself reflected here as the acme of civilization. And this, of course, was further reinforced in the visual encoding of the concerts themselves. As Erlmann argues, the use of dress as a 'metonymic gesture, as a spectacle within a spectacle' was a demonstration of the 'progressive history of the wearers' (Erlmann: 103).

Erlmann goes on to point out that the organisation of the photograph that accompanied the article reads like a trophy hunter's portrait (see Figure 2). The symmetrical positioning of the Choir for the camera, the placing of the two white men, the skins and (rather incongruously) a tiger's skin on the floor all reinforce the notion of 'the other' as chaotic nature, caught organised and ultimately tamed; a reassertion of the epistemology of modernity and progress within which the viewer/audience could assert their own identity.

However, as Erlmann reveals (pp. 103–104), this is a construction of the 'native' tailored to appeal to the Victorian audience and bearing little resemblance to clothes as worn in Africa. Many of the Choir are wearing woollen blankets, European imports to Africa as part of the trade in manufactured goods. They were gradually adopted in South Africa through the nineteenth century and, for the wearers, signified a very complex relationship with modernity, as much a sign of protest as one of acquiescence. A semiotic system is in operation between the members of the Choir themselves, which would not have been read by Europeans. There are other incongruities in this 'generic' African folk costume. The beads worn by some of the women closely resemble Victorian costume jewellery; the woman in the middle appears to be wearing some sort of western gown. Could it be that this 'bricolage of Victorian and African sartorial elements', to use Erlmann's phrase, demonstrates that 'the performers, like many other Africans involved in the emerging international show business', as Annie E. Coombes suggests, 'knowingly exploited a presentation of self and identity which re-appropriated and transformed anticipated western assumptions about the African and Africa and which was calculated to have a particular effect in Britain' (Coombes: 107)?

Preliminary stages of the African choir project

Much of the above has come from Erlmann's extensive research. A Small Grant from the Arts and Humanities Research Council in 2005 facilitated a programme of my own research in the United Kingdom and South Africa and established a network of contacts in South Africa interested in developing the story of the Choir for the stage. I organised the material I had gathered into a draft script and sent this to the Market Theatre Laboratory in Johannesburg. A positive response led to an invitation to conduct a two-week workshop with the students there.

5. By the latter part of the century, in keeping with the new industrial ethos, the 'assimilationist' policy had changed, and technical education was considered more appropriate for the African population (Saayman p.2).

The Market Laboratory is the training and developmental wing of the Market Theatre in Johannesburg. Vanessa Cooke, the current director of the Lab, traces its history:

> When Barney Simon was Artistic Director of the Market Theatre he always wanted a space where directors and actors could explore without having the pressure of producing a finished product, where there would be a right to fail. This dream stemmed from the fact that for years Barney had been doing workshop theatre under huge pressure as there had to be a product for the Market audiences.
>
> Also Community Theatre practitioners were coming to Barney to have their plays at the Market. These practitioners from the townships and rural areas were generally passionate about theatre but largely unskilled. Barney wanted to set up a Fieldwork programme to impart Theatre skills to the groups and to have a space where showcases could take place.
>
> He wanted also to have Drama Classes – initially for professional actors – but later when the pros were not enthusiastic – for young talented people from disadvantaged communities who had no chance of entering a tertiary institution either because of lack of funds or because of their grades at school.
>
> The Lab opened in October 1989 with seed money from the Rockefeller Foundation. (Cooke, personal interview, September 2006)

Currently the Market Lab offers young aspiring performers, from all over South Africa, the opportunity to engage in an intensive two-year course to develop their skills.

The rationale behind the structure of the workshop and subsequent presentation to an invited audience was driven by a number of different imperatives. It was necessary to determine how much was known about these late nineteenth-century pioneers by the current generation of performers in South Africa. The loosely formulated draft script used the narrative of the Choir's adventures as an organising device to explore the complex issues of representation and identity raised by the decision of the Choir to perform in 'traditional' costumes. It speculated about the extent to which the Choir may have constructed this identity specifically to appeal to Victorian audiences and *knowingly exploited* their audiences' expectations. It explored the changes this experience wrought on certain individual members of the group, what this cost them in human terms as they struggled with these conflicting versions of self. The workshop would determine whether or not these issues of representation and identity were of interest and relevant to contemporary South Africans working in the field of performance and other sectors of the cultural industry. As a writer and director I wanted to examine the ways in which the medium of performance itself might be used to explore the act of watching and being watched, both then and now, and be utilised as a means of interrogating the 'past' in the 'present'. The audience and audience response thus became a key

Jane Collins

factor in the research process and the workshop experiments, both in terms of form and content. It was these questions and propositions that were offered up for analysis through practice over the course of a two-week intensive workshop in Johannesburg in April 2006. The draft took the narrative up to the point of the Xinwines' departure from the tour in Manchester. The outcomes of the workshop and feedback from the audience in a post-presentation discussion would be used to develop the draft material into a full-length new work.

The collaborative team in South Africa consisted of eighteen second-year students from the Lab, together with Napo Masheane, director, Thembe Khubeka, musical director at the Lab, and Michael Pavelka, designer, from Wimbledon College of Art in the UK.

On the first day of the workshop, research material consisting of documents, books, newspaper articles, letters and photographs was laid out for the group to share. The script was introduced as a series of starting points to be developed through experimentation and play. The designer had brought out copies of the recently recovered Mitchell and Kenyon films of England at the dawn of the last century, slightly later than the Choir's visit in the 1890s but nonetheless evocative of working-class life in the northern industrial cities and towns. We watched some of these and compared the images with early pictures of Cape Town, Johannesburg and Kimberley. It became apparent that the students had little knowledge of urban life in nineteenth-century South Africa and that this world was as remote to them as the chimneys and factory smoke of industrial England.

A nation that loses awareness of its past gradually loses itself (Kundera: 235)

These aspects of the colonial past have quite literally been airbrushed out of South African history by apartheid education. The company had never heard of Charlotte Manye, a powerful advocate of Women's Rights who went on to become the first female Black African graduate of Wilberforce University in the United States. They had no idea about the existence of prominent intellectuals and businessmen like Paul Xinwine. The notion of a black educated middle-class elite at the end of the last century, many of whom had a vision of an autonomous, self-governing Black Nationalist state, was a complete revelation to the students. Indeed, as the discussion after the performance revealed, it was unknown to many of the audience members as well.

The students were all accomplished singers and work began each morning with a vocal warm-up and singing workshop led by Thembe Khubeka. Khubeka, herself a professional singer, has toured in Europe and America with a number of different South African choirs. Her experience as a black African performer on the contemporary world stage was invaluable to the workshop process. The concert repertoire of the African Choir consisted of a combination of hymns, traditional songs, Negro spirituals and English ballads. It was not the intention to reproduce these performances but to explore the ways in which music might be used as a discursive tool to highlight the tensions in the group as they struggled with the conflicting demands of the 'box office' and their own sense of identity.

The way in which they staged some of their songs is more concealed than revealed in the *Times* review of 3 July 1891: 'The wayside song and dance were very characteristic, and the wedding song, with its touches of dramatic effect caused much amusement'. Characteristic of what is difficult to ascertain, because the reviewer goes on to bemoan the fact that another one of the indigenous songs performed by the Choir 'bore so close a resemblance to Rossini's 'Cujus animam' that it is difficult to accept it as a specimen of native music at all'. This review then raises the issue of the sartorial representation of the Choir: 'it was no doubt desirable to qualify the strict accuracy of the native costumes but surely the harmonies need not have been Europeanised also'. The reviewer appears on the one hand to be demanding a more 'authentic' rendition of the African experience while on the other acknowledging that this must be kept within the bounds of the sensibilities of the Victorian audience.

As Erlmann points out, discourses around sartorial representation were, in the minds of Victorian audiences, inextricably linked to their view of the contemporary world, constituting, that is to say, a 'complacent metropolitan discourse about morals, markets, spiritual salvation and social distinctions'. Erlmann goes on to describe the ways in which the European missionaries had made clothing 'one of the most morally charged mediums of their message. By re-styling the outer shell of the 'heathen' they reasoned they would reform and salvage the inner self of the newly converted' (Lindfors: 126). Pavelka had brought to South Africa a number of Victorian-style corsets, made by the costume students at Wimbledon College of Art. In the first few days of the workshop the students explored the constraints and re-shaping of the body by the corset, on both male and female, and its effects on movement and codes of behaviour. Simple exercises involving standing, sitting and picking up objects off the floor evoked the strangeness of Victorian dress as worn by the black middle-class in the nineteenth century and revealed to the workshop performers what Foucault calls 'the political anatomy' or the 'mechanics of power' (Foucault: 138) on the colonial subject. For the workshop presentation these evocations were developed to suggest the ways in which the Victorian Choir might have understood these mechanisms. A scene that depicts the conflicting reactions of the Choir to the proposal that they should present themselves in 'native' dress to attract larger audiences, simultaneously reveals an understanding of the ways in which these codes might be exploited:

Eleanor Xinwine: It's too dangerous. Physically and morally dangerous.
Paul Xinwine: It's only a costume.
Eleanor Xinwine: I'm not wearing animal skins.

Sannie Koofman:	Make my flesh creep.
Josiah Semouse:	There's some blankets in the hotel, good colours, a bit like the Bantu women wear.
Sannie Koofman:	My people wouldn't wear those.
Eleanor Xinwine:	Nor would mine.
Paul Xinwine:	Your people aren't here. (Author's draft text)

In fact, news of the Choir's presentation of themselves in this fashion did eventually reach the Cape where it provoked outrage in the press, prompting one of the managers to write to the editor of the *Christian Express* on Christmas Day 1891 to refute the allegations of impropriety:

> . . . you sir are labouring under a very great misapprehension for I take it when you say that the costume is physically and morally dangerous you have come to the conclusion that the dress is worn as in Africa. It is not so. Due regard has been paid to the health and comfort of the natives and they simply wear their skins over their ordinary clothing.

There is an element of truth in this explanation, since, as described above, the dress certainly wasn't worn as in Africa; all that mattered was that it passed for what was worn in Africa in the minds of the spectator.

The extent to which the Choir may have been complicit in the construction of the mise-en-scène for the photograph that appeared in Stead's *Review of Reviews* (see Figure 2) was also suggested in the draft text:

Paul Xinwine:	One of the managers thinks he knows where he can locate a tiger skin.
Eleanor Xinwine:	What on earth for?
Paul Xinwine:	Create a bit of an atmosphere.
Josiah Semouse:	There are no tigers in South Africa.
Paul Xinwine:	There's no jungle either, but the English don't know that.

We were mindful that the comic potential of this scenario must not detract from the fact that the extent to which the end justified the means must have caused the Choir considerable anguish. In the workshop, through discussion and improvisation, the company explored a number of different versions of the scenario, with the students adopting different roles and positions for and against. It is interesting to note that the Choir's concert dress for the second half of the performance (one assumes they changed in the interval) consisted of white dresses and gloves for the ladies and tail-coats for the gentlemen, a reassuring assertion through sartorial representation of the values of late Victorian society.

The draft script was constructed around the stories of five members of the Choir. Charlotte Manye [Plate 4] and her younger sister Katie; Paul Xinwine and his wife Eleanor; Josiah Semouse, the young journalist who kept a diary of the tour, and the unfortunate Sannie Koopman who was

Plate 4: Kholosa Tshandana as Charlotte Manye.

described in the *Christian Express* in 1892 as 'the more sinned against . . . and for whom we are exceeding sorry'. All the other roles, including the English manager Balmer, Queen Victoria, the white pianist Miss Lillian Clark and Baroness Burdett-Coutts of the International Congress of Hygiene and Demography, who, in the Victorian philanthropic tradition, supported the Choir by sending them gifts of warm clothes and woollen stockings, were to be played by members of the company. The company also functioned as a chorus that commented on the action and the way the action was presented, calling on the audience to re-consider what it had just seen.

The notion of young black South African performers playing a range of white Victorian characters posed a series of interesting questions for the company. How do you represent 'the other' without caricature? How do you clearly delineate age and status without resorting to cliché? Simply and directly, how do you make it clear to the audience that at this point you are representing a person of another race on stage? Different solutions were found in relation to the 'function' of the different white characters in the drama. In the case of Miss Clark, the pianist, for example, in the workshop and in the presentation the Choir performed the songs unaccompanied: however, they performed them 'as if' there was a pianist in the wings. The influence Miss Clark exerted over the real choir on the actual tour, especially the girls, was considerable. In the workshop this influence was revealed through a series of anecdotes told by two of the male actors in the company. With the help of a large floral hat they 'performed' Miss Clark for each other while the 'real' Miss Clark remained offstage to be constructed in the imagination of the audience [Plate 5].

Plate 5: Thabang Kwebu as Miss Clark.

6. On 14 September 2006, Ms. N. G. W. Botha, Deputy Minister of Arts and Culture in South Africa, unveiled a commemorative plaque in honour of Mrs. Charlotte Makgomo Maxeke (née Manye) in Soweto.

Balmer, the English manager, was more difficult. He was a key figure in the narrative, requiring a strong 'presence' on stage, presented as someone caught between a genuine desire to support the Choir and the more mercenary demands of other members of the management committee. Thabiso Phetla stepped out of the chorus and, donning a cream Panama hat, announced to the audience that he was now playing the English manager Balmer. The 'hat as Balmer' was maintained as a presence on the stage even in those moments when Phetla re-joined the chorus. The combination of these Brechtian devices of direct address and the use of the chorus moved the narrative forward and maintained contact between the performers and audience throughout the dramatic action.

An early sequence that we developed in the workshop depicts the Choir on a sightseeing tour of London, taking in all the major places of historical interest. These outings always ended at one of the newly opened and highly fashionable department stores for 'shopping'. Dramatically, this pattern was built up by the chorus through a number of repetitive physical and vocal motifs, building up tension and expectation only for this to be punctured at the end of the last sequence by Charlotte who directly informs the audience: 'We didn't shop. We stood and watched and wondered at the great British public, shopping' [Plate 6].

Charlotte was a complex figure: Only recently acknowledged publicly for her contribution to human rights in South Africa she has been described as 'the mother of African freedom'.[6] In the workshop we explored the extent to which her views might have been shaped by her exposure to the radical elements of English society at the end of the nineteenth century. In *The Calling*

Katie Makanya
(née Manye) died
in 1955. Before
she died, Margaret
McCord, who was the
daughter of Dr James
McCord for whom
Katie worked for
35 years, recorded
her life story. Katie's
oral testimony
includes her travels
with the African
Choir, her marriage
on return to South
Africa, and continues
into the apartheid
years.

Plate 6: The company 'Shopping'.

of Katie Makanya,[7] Charlotte's younger sister Katie remembers being taken
with Charlotte on a visit to Russell Square to meet Emmeline Pankhurst.
Katie was shocked by Mrs Pankhurst's behaviour, describing her as someone
who 'spoke out her deep thoughts without any pretence of courtesy'
(McCord: 54). Mission-educated young black women of the nineteenth
century were not encouraged to have deep thoughts, let alone to voice them.

William Stead, the journalist who interviewed Charlotte for the article
in the *Review of Reviews* in September 1891, was a close friend of Annie
Besant. He was clearly impressed by Charlotte, describing her in the same
article as 'an expert linguist speaking no fewer than five or six languages'.
It is quite possible that he would have introduced her to his friend Annie
and to other English radicals both male and female. To what extent did this
highly intelligent strong-willed young woman from the Basotho people find
common ground and even common grievance with her English sisters?

Over the two weeks of the workshop the performers researched the lives of
the members of the Choir that were of particular interest to them, construct-
ing individual presentations from fragments of letters, newspaper articles and
the biographical accounts that the Choir themselves had provided to journal-
ists while on tour. These were presented in a combination of Xhosa, Zulu,
Sotho and English, the multilingual nature of the workshop drawing on the
diversity of the student group and reflecting the make-up of the original Choir.

The medium of instruction at the Lab is English and all the students
spoke it to an excellent standard. In the workshop we played with the
degree to which we might use heightened language to reflect the more
precise non-Americanised elocution of the Victorian middle classes. In the
short time available, however, the students found this restricting both in

terms of establishing relationships between the characters and the ongoing dialogue with the audience. We were not striving for historical reproduction or accuracy, so it was more appropriate that the students were comfortable in their delivery. However, the hegemonic influence of the English language as an instrument of imperial power was demonstrated through the following exchange. Balmer and Xinwine have just introduced the idea of traditional costumes. This is met with a silence of disbelief from the rest of the choir. After a moment Balmer speaks:

Balmer: Would you like me to withdraw so you can talk amongst yourselves?

Paul Xinwine: We can talk amongst ourselves with you in the middle of us.

The Choir members then attempt to have a conversation in their own voice as a means of re-asserting their African identity on their own terms. They reach into their past to argue whether or not their past should be represented. But communication breaks down as there are too many different languages among the group and because some of the younger members, for whom English has almost become a first language, can't find the words to express themselves in their mother tongue. The missionaries have done a good job; en masse the group can only communicate in the language of the coloniser. Balmer is asked to leave and the discussion continues in English.

Each evening, after discussions with Khubeka, Masheane and Pavelka, I re-shaped the draft, incorporating the material discovered through the workshop during the day and as a result of ideas presented by the students. As a rule, however, the experience of each day's workshop would result in long sections of text being expunged as the discourse inherent in the material asserted itself through dramatic action rather than words.

To control symbolic space is effectively to control the audience's reading of the event, and hence the meanings that may be discerned there.

Counsell and Wolfe: 156

The Laboratory Theatre is a black box with fixed end-on tiered seating. This spatial configuration re-creates the relationship of the Victorian spectator to the stage. Pavelka created a 'white' space within the box, in which the playing area was defined by a set of light bulbs that acted as footlights, a trunk and eighteen chairs. The workshop presentation was intended to be both illusionistic and counter-illusionistic, setting up a framework of production and reception that exploited the voyeuristic performance conventions of the proscenium arch only to undermine them.

London, August 1891, seated in the Royal Albert Hall are eighteen[8] young black South Africans. They are dressed in fashionable Victorian attire, the women straight backed and tight laced, the men in black jackets and waistcoats sit bolt upright listening to a performance of a work by Elgar. It is one of the hottest English summers in living memory. As the evening wears on a thousand gaslights are illuminated. Between movements there is a gentle

8. Eighteen students, in their final year at the Lab, participated in the workshop. We therefore expanded the number of choir members from the fifteen in the original African Choir.

Plate 7: Opening Scene: The Royal Albert Hall.

flutter of fans, a polite clearing of throats, a discreet dab of the handkerchief
to arrest the flow of perspiration on the forehead and down the back of the
neck before the next glissando on piano and strings sweeps and swirls
around the glass dome and up and out to the heavens beyond.

The stage directions above describe the opening sequence of the workshop
presentation, *The Story of the African Choir*, performed at the Market
Theatre Laboratory in Johannesburg on Friday, 7 April 2006, to an invited
audience. The Choir in their everyday Victorian clothes listen to Elgar in the
Albert Hall [Plate 7]. Architecturally, the interior of the Albert Hall means
that everybody is on display, the audience watches itself. The Choir thus
watches the audience watching them. The violins of Elgar are superseded by
'Ulo Tixo Omkulu' or the Great Hymn. Written by Ntsikana Gaba, considered to be one of the earliest Xhosa Christian converts, this hymn was sung
by the Choir in their original performances. For a few moments the voices of
the Choir and Elgar's violins co-mingle and then gradually the Elgar fades
and the 'unitary voice' of the Choir takes over. The performers look directly
at the contemporary audience across the footlights and construct them as a
nineteenth-century audience. They play on the assumptions and preconceptions of this 'constructed' nineteenth-century audience, taking their gloves
off in public, loosening their collars while simultaneously revealing current
perceptions and prejudices – thus the past and the present coalesce in the
theatrical moment. The performers control and direct the gaze of the audience back on itself, and in so doing they assert their own subject position as
the audience becomes the object of their gaze and scrutiny. How will they
read us? How do we read them? [Plate 8].

Jane Collins

Plate 8: Looking at the audience.

As the action progresses this unitary voice fragments under the social and financial pressures of the tour, and individual voices emerge with their different agendas. The strain of a heavy touring schedule took its toll on the health of the group. Conflicting objectives as to the purpose of the tour and the way in which they should present themselves opened up rifts between the Choir's members on issues of politics, ethics, gender and identity. These disputes highlight the paradoxical position of many performers from the continent of Africa on the world stage at the height of the colonial regime, who were required to construct themselves as the 'primitive' and the 'exotic other' to appeal to Victorian audiences. David Miller, in *The Myth of Primitivism* (pp. 50–71), describes the ways in which people can very quickly change the nature of what they produce in response to the presence of a ready market. Miller is describing the trade in cultural artefacts in the nineteenth century at the height of colonialism, and the resulting *primitivism* constructed jointly by colonised and coloniser to satisfy popular fantasies of imperial power. One cultural artefact not treated by Miller is performance. However, the tour was presented as a charitable venture, and the Choir were not strictly performers in the sense of music-hall entertainers or a travelling troupe trying to 'cash in' on popular fantasies. They saw themselves as representative of the black educated elite, epitomising the benefits of Christianity and modernity on the African continent. The English organizers, whose accounting was less than transparent, claimed over the course of the tour to have lost over one thousand pounds. To what extent can these losses be attributed to the Choir's failure to fulfil the preconceived notion of the 'African' in the mind of the Victorian audience?

The English pianist Miss Clark, in what was probably a well-intentioned attempt to defend Charlotte Manye's attack on Eleanor Xinwine, unfortunately only succeeded in re-affirming a tried and tested colonial strategy for writing off the behaviour of the colonised as infantile and illogical. She suggested to Manchester magistrates that the divisions that had blighted the progress of the Choir were the result of jealousy and tribal differences. Petty rivalries are common in all touring companies, but in this instance the arguments over who got the solos, who received the most gifts from the audience each night, living accommodation and food were the surface manifestations of far greater insecurities. The pressure of perpetually being expected to 'perform' a version of themselves that was the antithesis of everything they had been brought up to believe they were took its toll psychologically and emotionally on the group. The ways in which they negotiated that alienation and found their way out of it were very different for each member of the Choir and will form the basis for the next stage of the research.

Xinwine was in his mid-twenties at the start of the tour, but the average age of most of the Choir was around nineteen. Charlotte's sister Katie was only seventeen when she arrived in England. This group of young anglophile South Africans started out with such great expectations but gradually their faith in the fiction of modernity and progress had to confront the harsh realities of late Victorian society, manifested in the slums of the metropolis and the poverty of the rural communities they passed through on their travels. With diminishing funds and the pressure mounting on them to fulfil the expectations of the managers and their western audiences, while not offending the sensibilities of the mission-educated European and African elite back home in the Cape who had put their faith in them, is it any wonder that the group started to fragment under the strain, fight among themselves and eventually break up? It is no accident that years later, when the Nigerian writer Chinua Achebe gave a voice to the colonial subject, he chose a quotation from Yeats as the title of his first novel, *Things Fall Apart*.

Our investigation through performance of these hidden aspects of the colonial period speculates about the extent to which the black educated middle class in the late nineteenth century exercised agency and self-determination in terms of the ways in which they 'fashioned' their identity. In the post-colonial era the question remains as to the extent to which the mutual reinforcement of 'false' identities described by Erlmann has simply been re-configured as part and parcel of the traffic in global cultural commodities. This also resonates with current debates about identity in the new democracy of South Africa.

Sharon Cort, a documentary film maker based in South Africa, attended the workshop presentation of *The Story of the African Choir* and has included footage from it in her series 'New Conversations', which was broadcast on SABC in July 2006. In one of the programmes in the series, entitled 'Beyond the Rainbow', Steve Kwena Mokwena, a cultural activist, suggests that the problems facing the current generation of young South Africans as they attempt to assert/re-assert their identity are not so much the legacy of the white racist past but of finding ways of responding to 'the global deluge of ideas about what you are in a world that has reduced you to nothing but a consumer'. As a producer as well as a consumer, Gregory Maqoma, Director of the Vuyani Dance Theatre Project in Johannesburg,[9] in an unpublished paper delivered in South Africa in 2002 states, 'as a black African dancer, I am constantly expected to conform to stereotypical perceptions of the western world and of African traditionalists'.

9. Vuyani Dance Theatre Project. www.vuyani.co.za

The proliferation of image in a mediatised culture is one of the means by which narratives of power are maintained. In the face of these unitary and homogenised 'representations', live performance can either reinforce this hegemonic discourse or offer up alternative perspectives. *The Story of the African Choir* offers up the experiences of a past generation as they struggled to come to terms with the demands of 'the market' at the same time as retaining a sense of self. Strategically, while acknowledging it cannot step outside the politics of representation, the work attempts to use the medium of performance to offer up a critique of performance by exposing the complicit nature of the act of watching and being watched both under the colonial gaze and in the post-colonial world of global capitalism. At the time of writing, funds are being sought to develop the work in South Africa into a full-length performance that will include a programme of workshops for schools. Given the inter-cultural and collaborative nature of the research process, both on a theoretical level and in the practice-led workshop, it is to be hoped that the work will also eventually be seen in the West. It will then of course become part and parcel of the trade in cultural commodities, and the performers, like Gregory Maqoma, run the risk of being trapped in the same discourse as their nineteenth-century counterparts. However, the South African audience who attended the workshop presentation of *The Story of the African Choir* in Johannesburg affirmed its value as an important part of the process of re-claiming a hidden past and holding it up to scrutiny. If it is eventually seen by western audiences, it will offer them the opportunity to re-consider the colonial gaze and to reflect on the extent to which in the current world market, as the Zulu phrase puts it, Umuntu, Ngumuntu, Ngabantu. A person is a person through other persons or I am what I am because of you.

The Market Theatre Lab student ensemble
Thabo Flo Mokale, Nonhlanhla Kubheka, Paul Noko, Bongani Msibi, Kholosa Tshandana, Xolisa Mkafulo, Lehlohonolo Styx Mokejane, Thabang Kwebu, Thabiso Phetla, Onkaetse Vincent Maclean, Lebogang Inno, Pulane Jantjies, Kekeletso Matlabe, Millicent Makhado, Thobile Brenda Masemula, Thunyelwa Thambe, Nompilo Shazi, Tiny Kgamanyane.

Acknowledgements

To Vanessa Cooke and Dan Robbertse of the Market Theatre Lab and Jan Ryan, UK Arts International. This work was supported by an Arts and Humanities Research Council Small Grant and the Wimbledon College of Art. Plates 1 and 2 are reproduced from Margaret McCord, *The Calling of Katie Makanya*, by kind permission of New Africa Books. Plate 3 is reproduced from the Website of the New African Movement, by kind permission of Ntongela Masilela. Plates 4–6 are reproduced by kind permission of Michael Pavelka.

Works cited

Coombes, Annie E. (1997), *Re-inventing Africa*, New Haven and London: Yale University Press.

Counsell, Colin and Laurie Wolfe (eds.) (2001), *Performance Analysis*, London: Routledge.

Erlmann, Veit (1999), *Music, Modernity and the Global Imagination*, Oxford and New York: Oxford University Press.

—— (1999), 'Spectatorial Lust', in Bernth Lindfors (ed.), *Africans on Stage*, pp. 107–134.

Foucault, Michel (1991), *Discipline and Punish: The Birth of the Prison*, trans. Alan Sheridan, London: Penguin.

Kundera, Milan (1983), *The Book of Laughter and Forgetting*, London: Penguin.

Lindfors, Bernth (ed.) (1999), *Africans on Stage*, Cape Town: David Philip.

McCord, Margaret (1995), *The Calling of Katie Makanya*, Cape Town: David Philip.

Miller, David (1991), 'Primitive art and the necessity of primitivism to art', in S. Hiller (ed.), *The Myth of Primitivism: Perspectives on Art*, London, New York and Toronto: Routledge, pp. 50–71.

Shephard, Ben (2003), *Kitty and the Prince*, London: Profile Books.

Magazines and Periodicals

The Christian Express, South Africa, August 1892.

The Irish Times, 15 March 1892.

The Review of Reviews, September 1891.

South Africa, March and September 1892.

The Times, 3 July 1891.

Television

new conversations, a series by Sharon Cort broadcast on SABC July 2006, angel films, angel@global.co.za

Suggested citation

Collins, J. (2007), '"Umuntu, Ngumuntu, Ngabantu": The story of the African choir', *Studies in Theatre and Performance* 27: 2, pp. 95–114, doi: 10.1386/stap.27.2.95/1

Contributor details

Jane Collins is Reader in Theatre at the Wimbledon College of Art. She is a writer and director whose extensive links with African theatre include the co-direction in Kampala (Uganda) of *Maama Nalukela Ne'zzadde Lye* (1995), a version of *Mother Courage* which was the first official African translation of a play by Brecht. With Michael Pavelka, she is joint-curator of the exhibition 'Stages Calling' at the Royal National Theatre (March 2007). The exhibition marks thirty years of the history of the Market Theatre in Johannesburg.
E-mail:j.a.collins@wimbledon.arts.ac.uk

Studies in Theatre and Performance Volume 27 Number 2 © 2007 Intellect Ltd
Article. English language. doi: 10.1386/stap.27.2.115/1

'Going to the Centre': Edward Bond's *The Children*

David Allen

Abstract

Edward Bond argues that every play has a 'centre' – a basic problem or paradox, which 'it is difficult for the audience to disentangle'. The centre, for Bond, is always an extreme situation. 'Extreme', in this context, does not necessarily mean violent. Rather, extreme situations are those in which individuals have to make critical choices. The concept of 'centre' has a particular meaning in Bond's work. For him, the central problem of all drama is justice. He argues that we have a basic existential need for justice (which he terms our 'radical innocence'); but the societies we live in are unjust. This, for Bond, is the human dilemma; and in extreme situations, the antinomy is exposed. Bond goes so far as to argue that drama does not teach us about the need for justice; rather, we experience it. Faced with extreme situations, we have to make our own dialectical choice between justice and injustice, the human and the inhuman.

This paper interrogates the validity of Bond's arguments. It is argued that extreme situations do not function, as he claims, to reveal some basic human need for justice. Rather, Bond's purpose is didactic. He is using a range of techniques to teach us about 'the need of justice'. The paper focuses, in particular, on his play The Children *(2001), which was written to be performed by a cast of young people, working with two adult actors. Semi-improvised, it is designed to put young people through 'extremes of experience', and put them in 'fundamental, searching situations'. A production of* The Children *was staged by Midland Actors Theatre in 2004–2005. The paper looks at how the company worked on the play in rehearsal. It draws on extensive interviews and discussions with cast members, as well as on unpublished letters and materials by Bond.*

Keywords

Edward Bond
The Children
extreme situations
radical innocence
aggro effects

Edward Bond argues that every play has a 'centre' – a basic problem or paradox, which 'it is difficult for the audience to disentangle; often because there is no single right solution' (Bond 2003d). The centre, for Bond, 'is always an extreme situation. . . . It is probably a situation, a confrontation, that is not solvable. And the structures of the play will gravitate towards being extreme exposures of that Central situation' (Bond, cited Stuart 1994: 137) 'Extreme' in this context does not necessarily mean 'violent'. Bond has defined extreme situations as those in which individuals have to make critical choices – when they 'seem to have no chance of expressing their humanity, except perhaps at great cost' (Bond 1995: 156, 157). Take, for example, the moment when Antigone, in Sophocles' play, accepts imprisonment and death, rather than obey a law she does not believe in.

1. Unless otherwise specified, all quotations from French texts have been translated by Stephanie Terpant, specially for this paper.

(She dies, she says, 'Unjustly, for upholding justice/And the humanity of humankind' – Sophocles 1994: 171, 172.) She makes a critical choice, and at great personal cost. In making this choice, she crosses a threshold or barrier.

In extreme situations like this, says Bond, 'the contradictions in being human become critical' (Bond 2004a: 28). Two necessities, 'that of acting as a human being and that of acting as a social being, meet and clash' (Bond 2001c: 145).[1] The spectator has to ask him or herself: 'What would you do in this situation?' (Bond 2001b: 45).

Justice

It is evident that the notion of the 'centre' has a *particular* meaning in Bond's work. He argues that the central problem of all drama is justice. Writing about his play *In the Company of Men*, he observed that

> it takes the audience on a journey across the cultural, political barriers to justice and understanding – and their counterparts in our psychologies. . . . All drama takes such a journey in its search for justice. If the journey is well taken, we understand justice better and so our desire for it is greater (Bond 2001a: 17).

Bond believes that we are born 'radically innocent'. This is the newborn child's desire to be at home in the world, 'and that requires that the world be a home'. Later, this becomes a desire that the world should be 'a place of peace and justice' (Bond 2004a: 25), the 'shared home of all people' (Bond n.d., a).

The need for justice, then, is a human imperative that begins in the infant. You cannot say that it is innate, Bond observes, 'but it is about as innate as anything can be in the mind' (Bond 2002). Society, however, is based on inequality and injustice:

> However much the child needs a just world, in growing up to survive in this world, he has to become part of an unjust world. This creates a conflict within him. So justice is transformed into revenge because the child is angry. The need for justice becomes the need for vengeance or injustice. It's a difficult idea. How can we kill people, when we want to be just? People are not unjust because they decide to be, they become unjust because they need to be (Bond 2004d: 22).

Elsewhere, however, Bond suggests that it is *society* that corrupts our need for justice, and turns it into the desire for revenge:

> Revenge is what society calls justice . . . we live in a society that desires revenge. The problem with revenge is that we cannot satisfy it, never, and societies that are driven by the desire for revenge become more and more destructive (Bond 2001c: 140).

Radical innocence may be corrupted, 'socially misappropriated and misused' (Bond 1998a: 257), but it is never wholly lost or suppressed: 'Ultimately – and I suppose this is a theoretical statement because I don't quite know how you demonstrate it – ultimately I think it is impossible for people to lose their innocence' (Bond 2003d). Even in our corrupted state, our unconscious 'sees through us' and 'sends us messages of our humanity' (Bond 1998a: 250). Innocence and corruption 'constantly dramatically agon-ise' in our minds (Bond 2005c). Bond argues that extreme situations expose this basic antinomy, and reveal our 'innocence'.

In 1983, Bond undertook a series of drama workshops with students at the University of Palermo.[2] He devised a scenario for an improvisation. It was based on an extreme situation: A soldier is given an order to perpetrate an inhuman act. He/she is told to take a baby from the street where they live, and kill it. Two babies live in the street: Their own mother's, and a neighbour's. The students who took part, then, had to consider: 'What would you do in this situation?' Each time one of them played the scene, they chose to kill their own brother, rather than the neighbour's child. Bond himself had anticipated that this would happen. The students, however, were perplexed. The improvisation had confounded all their expectations. As John Doona has observed:

> The Palermo Improvisation describes the uncovering of a paradox in which the human individual acts in a manner, which, to the understanding of the world, should be impossible. We all know that 'Blood is thicker than water' and that 'We look after our own'. Clearly the soldier will kill the neighbour's child to save his own sibling. But the paradox is unavoidable. If we are even surprised ourselves at the answer that we have given, what is the source of our answer? (Doona 2005: 97).

In the improvisation, the students had to choose between innocence and corruption; and, Bond claims, it changed them (Bond 2004c). 'What I think appears in the "Palermo Paradox"', he asserts, 'is the mind's insistence on its own nobility, its own integrity – that is its shared human-ness' (Bond 2001a: 185). In other words: It revealed our basic need for justice.

Bond used the Palermo improvisation as the central situation in *Red, Black and Ignorant* (1985) (part of the *War Plays* trilogy). A soldier has been ordered to kill someone in his street; he chooses to kill his own father, rather than a neighbour. One of the characters comments:

Why did he kill his father and not the stranger?
For all of us there is a time when we must know ourself.
No natural laws or legal codes will guide us.
Notions of good and evil will say nothing.
We know ourself and say: I cannot give up the name of human.
All that is needed is to define rightly what it is to be human.

2. Bond was a visiting professor at the University of Palermo in Sicily in 1983. (See Stuart 2001: x.)

If we define it wrongly we die.

If we define it and teach it rightly we shall live (Bond 1998b: 38).

In 'extreme' situations, then, we have to decide for ourselves 'what it is to be human'.

The 'paradox' in Bond is 'the sudden, dramatic assertion of radical innocence when it is confronted by a conflict between itself and social teaching, which social teaching cannot reconcile or conjure away' (Bond 1998a: 258). This paradox is at the centre of Bond's theatre. The aim of drama, he believes, should be to create situations (like the Palermo improvisation) in which the paradox reveals itself. 'I try to confront each member of the audience with their radical innocence,' Bond argues.

> I intend my plays to put each member of the audience on the spot – to say you are in this situation and that (I try to make it unavoidable) you must choose and your choice will define you . . . I think if you take responsibility for any serious situation – which makes serious demands on you – then you are taking responsibility for the world (Bond n.d., b).

Bond argues that drama cannot teach 'anymore than a statue can breathe' (Bond 2003c). An author should not provide answers; rather, the audience must find its own answers to the problems of 'humanness'. The tools of drama, Bond suggests, 'may be used for teaching such things as not to take drugs'; but this 'is limited to advising, cajoling, warning'. But the need for justice 'is asserted only in the extreme, its [sic] then that drama enacts the logic of humanness. It is enactment, not a lesson' (Bond n.d., d). If Bond is right, then, drama does not *teach* us about the need for justice. Rather, we *experience* it. We confront the 'tragic agon' between innocence and corruption. In extreme situations, we experience again the need for justice, to make the world a shared home for all. We escape the bounds of social teaching. Our 'unconscious' tells us (as Doona suggests), not that 'we look after our own', but that 'we cannot create our happiness on another's suffering' (Doona 2005: 98). In these circumstances, we may choose corruption – but if we do so, we must do it 'knowingly' (Bond 2004c). But is this naïve?

The existence of 'radical innocence' cannot be proved. It is a purely speculative construction. Bond insists that the concept is based in 'existential logic' (Bond n.d. a), but to assert this is no proof. In fact, the only real evidence he offers is the reaction of students to the Palermo improvisation; but this is shaky at best. The dilemma Bond presented to the students was simple and stark: They could kill one child, or the other. For Bond, it seems, one choice was 'corrupt'; the other was 'innocent'. One choice defined 'rightly' what it means to be human; the other would define it 'wrongly'. Bond claims, in fact, that the students 'got it right!' – i.e., 'they did not make the conventional decision' (Bond 2004d). But this statement, in itself, implies a value-judgement. The idea that the choice the students made was a manifestation of radical innocence is simply Bond's own subjective interpretation of what happened. It might be argued that our actions, in a situation like this, would be influenced by a complex range of factors. (For example, killing a child would produce feelings of guilt and shame; it might be that sacrificing a sibling, rather than a neighbour's child, might in some small measure reduce that guilt.) How, then, can we say for certain which action is 'innocent' and which is 'corrupt'?

'Aggro effects'

The Palermo improvisation was based on the idea of an extreme choice. We may distinguish another kind of 'extreme situation' in Bond's work, which functions differently – but which is also designed to reveal the 'tragic agon' between innocence and corruption.

Bond has developed a technique known as the 'aggro effect'. This is defined by Georges Bas as an act of theatrical provocation, which implicates the audience by '*demanding* an emotional response'. The purpose is to get a reaction, but further, to start a thought process about the *significance, the meaning*, of what is taking place . . .' (Bas 2005: 201). Bond argues that the shock of the 'aggro effect' is justified 'by the desperation of the situation or as a way of forcing the audience to search for reasons in the rest of the play' (Bond, cited Innes 1982: 200) Our emotional response means that we cannot 'evade the problem' (Bond 2003d).

'Aggro effects', then, involve shock, crisis and rupture. We are not presented with a choice; rather, we are forcefully confronted with a problem, which we have to try to understand and resolve. We can see how this works in Bond's play, *Olly's Prison* (1993). In the first scene, a man, Mike, harangues his daughter, Sheila, for some forty-five minutes, because she will not drink a cup of tea he has made her. Finally, he kills her. The murder is the 'Central Situation'. It 'creates a problem for the audience which is pursued throughout the play' (Bond 1996b: 14). We do not understand why he should kill her over a cup of tea; for any audience, 'that reason is insufficient' (Bond 2004c). We have to ask ourselves: 'Why?' ('Drama wants to give you the question "why?" and make you responsible for answering it' – Bond 2002). The murder, in fact, points to a contradiction, a conflict in Mike. This is how the action is described in the script:

> Mike slams his hands round Sheila's neck, lifts her straight up out of the chair and strangles her. For a moment she is too shocked to react. Then her hands go up and claw at his hands. Her body wrenches round once so that it is sideways to the table – the chair comes round with her. The shape of her body is contained in his body as if they were one piece of sculpture. The struggle is concentrated and intense – their bodies shake, vibrate, violently judder . . . Her hands claw more weakly, they seem to be patting his hands. No sound except breathing (Bond 1993: 11).

Mike kills in vicious anger; but this is part of his inner contradiction. Bond notes: 'Since the father does not hate his daughter I make the killing a birth image (he is pregnant with his daughter as he kills her)' (Bond 1996b: 14). The image creates, then, a paradoxical combination of tenderness and violence. It is the *Grundgestus* of the play, in the sense of embodying the central conflict, the central 'problem'. There is an unexpected – paradoxical – identity or superimposition of opposites; and this creates a gap in meaning, which the audience has to interpret.

In many ways, this 'aggro effect' is the *inverse* of the 'Palermo paradox'. In scenes based on the Palermo model, the individual is presented with a choice; in making that choice, they free themselves from social teaching, and discover their 'innocence'. Here, however, the action reveals the way the character is trapped, rather than free. The problem, the conflict, is locked inside Mike; subsequently, he has to struggle to free himself.

For Bond, the moment embodies and enacts 'the modern paradox' (Bond 2000f: 19). Mike tries to understand what has happened; he 'wants to know how it is that he could be in this position'. He 'has to think about *murder*'. He 'doesn't understand these problems' – i.e., he doesn't know how it is possible for human beings to kill; and 'the only thing he can do is keep pressing and pressing at the problem' (Bond 1994). Bond suggests that Mike has to seek the answers *outside* himself; he has to 'try to find what is out there that is the real force of destruction' (Bond 1994). In other words, the source of the paradox lies 'out there' in society. Mike is searching for his freedom and innocence 'in the face of the violence ideologically installed in society' (Bond 2005b: 89).

Bond has stated that his aim in the play was to demonstrate that the forces of 'Law and Order' in society are 'not humanizing' (Bond 1994). He attempts to make the audience follow the same journey as Mike – to look for the 'real' sources of violence. He does this by presenting us with problems and paradoxes to solve. At one point, for example Mike declares he did not murder his daughter. As Bond observes, we might expect him to say, 'I can't believe I killed her', or 'I don't know why I killed her' (Bond 1994); but instead he baldly states that he did not kill her, provoking us to ask 'Why?'.

Sheila had a boyfriend, Frank, who is a police officer. Frank seeks to punish Mike for what happened. In other words, he shows how the desire for justice can be turned into the desire for vengeance. For Mike, he becomes the embodiment of the violence 'out there', in society. In the play's final scene, he declares:

> Mike: I've got some of the answers now. Frank murdered my daughter . . .
> 'E wasn't there when it 'appened—didn't 'ave to be. 'E did it . . . 'Ow can I
> make anyone understand that? See the connections? They cant [*sic*]. That's
> why we go on sufferin (Bond 1993: 69–70).

Again, this is paradoxical. Mike finds some of the answers – but he does not spell them out for us. Instead, we are again presented with a puzzle to resolve. We have to try to make the connections ourselves.

Peter Palitszch – who staged the play at the Berliner Ensemble in 1994 – questioned the way Mike declares that it was Frank who killed his daughter. He observed:

> In German, we would say Frank was the murderer 'in reality'. We wouldn't say he killed her, because that is nonsense, but we would say 'in reality' or 'if you look beneath the surface' etc. We would try to express the difference between these two levels (Palitzsch 1994)[3].

3. Translated from the German by David Allen.

Bond however insisted that this would be 'doing the audience's work for them' (Bond 1994). In other words, he wanted audiences to find their own answers.

Nevertheless, it might be argued that, in presenting us with these puzzles and paradoxes, Bond already has the 'right' answers in mind. The fact that we have to solve the puzzle and complete the meaning for ourselves does not mean that the drama is not designed to teach. Underneath the play there is a simple schema, and a simple message. We are, like Mike, supposed to search for our innocence 'in the face of the violence ideologically installed in society'.

Despite Bond's insistence that plays cannot teach, there is, in fact, a central didactic intention running through his work. His drama does not enact; it demonstrates. It is designed to *teach* us 'what it is to be human'. Ultimately, he offers a simple solution to the 'paradox of humanness': We must make the world a better place.

The audience must take responsibility for the world. The ultimate definition of being human is that you take responsibility for the world you live in. You have to live these situations in such a way that they become creative, not destructive, and they leave behind a piece of freedom that would enhance the freedom of all (Bond 2004d: 21).

Performing Bond: *The Children*

In recent years, in his work in the UK, Bond has concentrated on writing for young people – because, he believes, 'children are still very close to the centre' (Bond 2000c).

> Children ask the profoundest questions. Children ask: What is justice? Why is our society violent and vengeful? They can respond to the sorts of problems and situations that I feel it is necessary to write about, for the common good . . .
>
> Children know what is happening, they know the world is violent and vengeful. The responsibility of the writer is to tell the truth of extreme situations (Bond, cited Gold 2000: 10).

Young people, Bond suggests, are often confronted in their own lives with extreme situations that demand answers. Growing up in a hostile environment, 'you have to ask yourself pretty quickly, "What's my life about? How do I survive?" You have to find resources within yourself. It is more dangerous and more human' (Bond, cited Gold 2000: 10). Young people, moreover, are 'close to the centre' because they have not yet been fully 'corrupted'. They are 'deeply involved in the problems of humanness and not yet in those of surviving in the economy' (Bond n.d., d).

> The creativity of the young is necessarily raw. But given our older confusion, this rawness is less damaging than our later discriminations. The rawness is radical, it comes from radical innocence – sometimes, with the young, in its last illuminations before it is immolated in the garish disciplined radicalism of revenge (Bond 2004b).

It may be argued that Bond's view of young people is somewhat idealised; but he denies this. He argues:

> I am not a romantic where young people are concerned. I can be working with them one day and everything's fine, then the next day they'll break all the windows of the cars in the neighbourhood. I don't defend that, I don't find that romantic . . . But they are sensitive to these questions. They will be obliged to learn to forget them for the most part, to learn to survive. And the arts of survival are always the arts of destruction (Bond 2001b: 43).

Bond's play *The Children* (2000) is written to be performed by a cast of young people, working with two adult professional actors. In the play, a young boy, Joe, is pressured by his mother to burn down a house. She will not explain why. He agrees; but another boy dies in the fire. Joe and his friends decide to run away. Suddenly, it is as if there is an apocalypse or environmental disaster: Everyone in the world disappears, except Joe and his Friends. They are carrying with them a stranger, an injured man. Unbeknown to them, he is the father of the boy who died in the fire. He is seeking revenge. He murders the children, one by one; until finally, only Joe is left alive, to face the future alone.

According to Bond, the centre of *The Children* is 'the journey for, to humanness' (Bond 2000b). It is about growing up and accepting 'responsibility for ourselves and others' (Bond n.d., c). In other words, it is about making the world our shared home. Joe's journey is like a rite of passage – 'the very ancient journey that all humans have had to go on since we first wanted to understand ourselves and take responsibility for our world' (Bond 2000a: 3). Bond hopes that, for the young people taking part in the play, the experience itself will be a 'journey', a 'rite of passage' that may help them to understand themselves and their world. The play, he observes, 'wants to involve the young people more deeply in the meaning of their own lives'. (Bond 2003c)

David Allen

Bond told one theatre company working on the play: 'I know that if we can take the young actors to the centre, the drama *will* be profound' (Bond 2000c). The play puts young people 'into fundamental, searching situations' – in other words, 'extreme' situations – 'which, in one way or another, at some time everyone must face. Our humanity depends on how we act in those situations, and the way we answer the questions they provoke' (Bond, cited Singer 2000).

Most of the scenes in *The Children* are improvised. In the text, Bond indicates what the characters might say, but he expects the young cast 'to improvise on the indications, both in rehearsals and performances. If they don't, the performance cannot work' (Bond 2003b). The fact that the dialogue is improvised means, to some extent, that the cast has to experience the drama themselves. They are put on the spot – as the students were in the Palermo improvisation. They are placed in situations, and have to react to the dilemmas the characters face. Eric Duchâtel comments:

> The young people involved find themselves doubly confronted by the fundamental situations that the drama proposes: eating, drinking, sleeping, protecting themselves, but also helping each other and helping another, the stranger; surviving. Doubly, because they are confronted by the fable that is given to them and the audience by the author, but also by the implication of their own words, brought into play with the words of others (Duchâtel 2006: 125).

The MAT production

In 2004–2005, Gillian Adamson and I co-directed a production of *The Children*, for the Midland Actors Theatre (MAT). Before we began working on the play, we tried to clarify for ourselves the problem or paradox at its 'centre'. Bond juxtaposes extreme opposites in the play. There is a dialectic and tension between caring and destruction. These opposites, in fact, seem to be dangerously intertwined. In the first scene, for example, Joe stands alone on stage. He holds a large puppet or doll, a relic of his childhood, and talks to it, as a child might talk to its toy. We learn that he has decided to get rid of the puppet. 'Why do I drag you around?' he says. 'It's got to stop! I'm too old for you! . . . I'll have to kill you' (Bond 2000e: 5–6).[4] At one point, he picks the puppet up, and swings it playfully from side to side; a moment later, he hits it repeatedly with a brick:

> Can't give you away to someone who doesn't care! (*Hits the puppet with the brick.*) Can't leave you on a bus! (*Hits the puppet with the brick.*) Someone might find you – who didn't humiliate you! (*Hits the puppet with the brick.*) Didn't hurt you! (p. 7).

Arguably, the stoning of the puppet is the central situation of *The Children*. It creates a problem for the audience, which is pursued throughout the play.

4. All subsequent page references to *The Children* are incorporated in the text.

5. See Bond 2005a: 7.

Joe loves the puppet one moment, and abuses it the next. Violence and caring are juxtaposed. The sudden switch from one extreme to another is an 'aggro effect': it provokes an emotional reaction in us. We then have to try to understand and explain this collision of 'opposites'. The stoning of the puppet embodies the central 'problem' in the play; it is the *Grundgestus*. Like the moment when Mike murders his daughter in *Olly's Prison*, it is an exposition of a 'contradictory internal process' (Brecht 1964: 54).

It seems that Joe can only get rid of the puppet through an act of violence, because that is what he has been taught: He abuses the puppet, and loves it, just as he is himself abused and loved by his mother. ('Anything goes wrong in our house,' he says, 'Mum hits me' – p. 6.) In the behaviour of the adults in the play, we can see 'the emotional and physical violence that is often used against young people' (Bond 2000a: 3). In his notes, however, Bond stresses that the adults are destructive 'because they love and need love'. The Mother uses and abuses Joe, because she herself has been exploited and abused. She desperately needs Joe to love her; and it is her need for love 'that makes her destructive'. The Man loses his son in the fire; in his case, love makes him destructive, because the loss 'causes him so much pain' (Bond n.d., c). The desire for justice is entangled with desire for revenge. In one of the play's final scenes, he sits among the children as they sleep. He looks at them, and says: 'If it was different we'd be friends. Take care of you. Treat you as mine.' He cradles a brick, and strokes it as if it is a baby. 'My son my son . . .', he says; and then, suddenly, he turns to the side, and kills one of the children with a blow of the same brick (p. 48). This recalls Joe's sudden attack on the puppet in scene one. Again, the moment shows two extremes, of caring and violence, combined in the same person, and physicalised in contrasting actions.

The play, then, in part reflects the way the adults mistreat and abuse young people. But Bond shows that violence is not simply an external threat: the seeds of destructiveness are present in the young people themselves. Bond has stated that the scene where Joe bricks the puppet relates to an actual murder.[5] It seems likely he is referring to the murder of Jamie Bulger. There are echoes, at least, of the Bulger case: the opening scene is set on wasteland by a railway track; a young boy (the puppet) is 'killed' with bricks.

The Bulger case provoked troubling questions about young people's capacity for violence, and the supposed erosion of 'childhood innocence' in contemporary society. Bond, however, argues: 'The problem with children is that the world of the adults into which they're being inducted is so cruel, arbitrary and absurd' (Bond 1998c: 24). If we could understand the child's mind,

> we would see that there are necessary tensions in it, unavoidable conflicts even in a good world, and even more so in our damaged and dangerous world (with its fantasies and injustices): and we would see that it is possible to enable children to experience their conflicts, to make them speak and not be bewildered and frustrated by emotional conflicts. This is the job of

David Allen

humane education: Education has, of course, to equip children to live in the world – but it should also enable the child to live sanely with itself (Bond 1998c: 26).

A humane education would enable the child 'to possess itself – own itself by becoming responsible for its own conflicts' (Bond 1998c: 27). Arguably, this is, in part, what Bond is attempting to do in *The Children* – especially through the character of Joe. Joe's conflicts are with the adult world, but also with himself:

> It is not enough for him to simply blame his mother for her violence. He has to know that she is violent – but that violence has also been nurtured in him . . . That is the whole point of the play (Bond 2000c).

In other words, he has to overcome his own inner conflict, and rediscover his innocence, in the face of the violence installed in society.

In *The Children*, the dilemmas the characters face centre on questions of caring and destruction. In Scene 5, for example, after Joe has burnt the house down, the Friends gather round him, to find out what he plans to do next. Then, the Man enters. He collapses on the ground; and they have to decide what to do with him.

> Friends   Can't leave him here.
> He'll be dead in the morning
> Sod him that's his fault! Leave him! (p. 29)

They decide to carry him with them, as they set off on their journey. In a sense, Bond has 'trapped' the characters – and the young people in the cast – by giving them a problem they have to deal with. They have to care for this stranger. Bond comments: 'I think that its (*sic passim*) natural for the young people in the play to argue whether or not they should help the Man – but its only by helping him that they can become themselves and help each other' (Bond n.d., c).

In the play, the children seem to become more mature than the adults. On the journey, they have to look after the Man, feed him and nurture him back to health. He is like a child they have to care for. (In one scene, they even have to teach him to walk.) In Scene Six, when some of the Friends want to get rid of the Man, Joe insists: 'We can't leave him now! There's no one else. He'd die.' (p. 32). He later observes: 'After all this, if we could walk off and leave someone to starve to death – what's the point of anything? If there was only me left – I still wouldn't leave him.' (p. 40). Joe, then, turns his own suffering into caring for the Man. The responsibility he feels for someone's death is converted to a sense of responsibility for a life. Bond argues that he survives, in the end, 'by refusing to betray – abandon – his own sense of himself when dealing with that which is the greatest risk to him: the stranger' (Bond 2003c).

6. Bond has described
a production of *The
Children* in a
Bucharest prison. The
young man cast as
Joe was in prison for
murder. At the first
rehearsal, he came
on stage with the
puppet – but found
he could not say his
lines: 'It was as if the
puppet was the body
of the person he had
murdered. In killing
the puppet, he would
be committing the
murder again.'
Another prisoner took
the puppet from him,
and said: 'I'll be the
puppet. Talk to me.'

The murderer
talks. He tells
the prisoner how
he will kill him.
He tries to tell him
why. He argues
with himself
and reaches a
conclusion. . . . He
said 'Now I must
kill you – because
that is what I did.'

Then the prisoner
suddenly jumped to
the end of the play,
where Joe is forgiven
by the ghost of the
boy he murders in the
fire: 'He said "And
before I kill you you
must forgive me." The
other prisoner said "I
forgive you" and the
rehearsal went on.'
Working on the scene
helped the young
man to become
responsible for his
own 'conflicts'. For
just long enough 'he
wore his victim's
shroud, and then he
murdered for the first
time'. He had never
seen a play, and yet,
Bond argues, he used
the drama as 'a
human resource'; he
had 'dramatised the
situation so that he
could find his
innocence' (Bond
2005: 7–8). Again,

There are two antithetical journeys in the play. Joe's journey is a rite of passage to adulthood. The Man, on the other hand, is like a child, who goes through the stages of growing up, but becomes 'very destructive'; the desire for revenge turns him ultimately into 'a beast, a crazy animal'. He represents, in part, 'the presence of potential dangerousness of a child becoming an adult' (Bond 2003d). In this way, in the characters of Joe and the Man, the play embodies the choice between innocence and corruption, humanness and inhumanness.

Behind the question of caring and destruction in *The Children* lies the question of justice, and the need to make the world a 'shared home for all'. Bond told a group in Beirut, which was working on the play:

> Some might tell you this here isn't your house, or this here isn't your book, or these here are not your clothes. They might tell you that many things are not yours. They cannot tell you that this world is not yours. This world is yours. A time will come when the people who tell you what is yours and what isn't will have left this world. But you won't have, and you will have to make it a place of kindness and peace. To take responsibility for the world, you must be courageous, generous and far-sighted. Performing *The Children* is a way to prepare for it. You must make this play yours, so the audience may understand what you want to tell them (Bond 2006: 127).

In a sense, Bond has here shown his hand. His purpose in the play is didactic. As we have seen, he hopes that the play will serve as a 'rite of passage' for the young people who perform it. In other words, his aim is to take them through the same learning process as the characters. He wants to prepare young people to 'take responsibility for the world' – to teach them about the need 'to replace revenge with justice, anger with care. Children must learn this, for all our sakes' (Bond, cited Gold 2000: 10).

Bond insists that drama cannot teach; and yet, as we will see, the 'extreme situations' in *The Children* are *learning situations*, designed to teach young people 'what it is to be human'.[6]

The play in rehearsal

We undertook two tours of *The Children*. At each venue, we rehearsed the play for a week with a group of some twenty young people. At the end of the week, the play was performed.[7]

There are a number of unexplained events in *The Children*. The play seems designed, in fact, to repeatedly provoke the question: 'Why?' Again, the audience (or in this case, the participants) have to complete the meaning. The young people we worked with found this frustrating at times. Holly Wright (Walsall College) observed: 'it's very puzzling and confusing, which is great because it makes everyone interested in it.' Hayley White said: 'I hate things like this, and love it too, because it keeps me awake at night, trying to work it out.'

We found a similar reaction in some audiences. At Egerton Park College, an audience of Year 9 pupils was left with numerous questions about the play; for example: 'Where do all the people go?' 'Was that man killing people 'cos they killed his son?' 'Where did the puppet come from?' One said that the play 'didn't add up; it was all in bits'.

Bond has observed:

> A play must not deliberately confuse but it should always open more doors than were open when it began . . . All I can do is record certain facts, say what events are known to have occurred . . . but that does not give the meaning of the facts. Meanings must be given by young people to facts which demand understanding – and in giving these meanings the young people create their humanity (Bond 2003c).

But Bond is doing more than simply recording 'certain facts'. Every 'gap' in meaning in the play is a *provocation*; a learning tool, designed to make us work on the question, 'why?'

Throughout the rehearsal process, we invited groups to air any questions they had about the play – and find their own answers. The question which groups asked more than any other was: 'Why does everyone else in the world disappear?' There is no simple explanation offered in the play. Bond notes that he wanted to evoke a sense of what it would feel like for young people to be suddenly lost and abandoned in a hostile world.

> The play wants to create a sense of desolation and abandonment, which all children at some time feel – but in which they do not despair but turn back to life, seek their maturity (Bond 2003c).

The change that occurs is psychological rather than 'literal' – an event in the psyche.

The learning point here is clear. Bond wants to teach young people about what it is like to feel 'you're on your own in the world' – to make their own decisions, and find their own explanations for things, without the guidance of adults. They have to become 'responsible for the world'.

In some ways, the experience of working on the play, for the young people involved, parallels the characters' experience. They, too, are thrown into a new situation, where they may feel disoriented, without their usual points of reference, and where they have to find answers and solutions for themselves. Our challenge in rehearsal was to 'start a thought process' about the significance of events, and to encourage young people to work on the level of 'meaning' rather than the level of 'facts'. For example, in trying to explain why everyone in the world disappears, some of them suggested that 'the children must be hallucinating', or 'it's all a dream that Joe has'. Others saw beyond this, however, and gave meaning to the 'facts'. Lewis Farricker (Egerton Park School) said that 'in their minds, the Friends are on their own'; and Amber Regan (William Brookes School) observed: 'There is

however, this is simply Bond's own subjective interpretation. It might be argued that what occurred was a form of drama therapy, rather than a manifestation of 'radical innocence'.

7. There were two MAT tours of *The Children*. The venues and performance dates were:

2004:

12 November: Castle Vale artSites, Birmingham

19 November: Halesowen College, Halesowen

26 November: High Arcal School, Sedgley

3 December: Vera Fenn Studio, Blue Coat School, Walsall

10 December: Toot Hill School, Bingham

17 December: Elizabethan High School, Retford

2005:

4 November: Summerhill School, Kingswinford

11 November: Egerton Park College, Manchester

18 November: Edge Arts Centre, William Brookes School, Much Wenlock

25 November: Washwood Heath Technology College, Birmingham

2 December: Halesowen College, Halesowen

9 December: Walsall College of Arts & Technology, Walsall

The company worked at each venue for five days prior to the performance, rehearsing the play with a group of students.

no one for them to rely on, because you're on your own in the world when you leave home.' Similarly, Russ Gibbs (Halesowen College) commented:

> What I think Bond is trying to bring across is, that every child goes through that kind of progression through life, like Joe, where he's figuring he doesn't need anybody, he can do it on his own; and then most of us snap out of it, and feel, 'Yes, we do need our parents' – but we try to push them away.

Choices

As we have seen, Bond claims the play puts young people in 'fundamental, searching situations' (Bond, cited Singer 2000). They find solidarity and discipline in 'the urgency the play's situations have for them'. But for that to happen, 'the situations must be made radically clear' (Bond 2003b). In other words, it is necessary to clarify what is at stake at any moment, and the choices that have to be made. In Scene 3, for example, Joe tells the Friends that he is going to burn the house down, as his mother wishes. They all swear a pact to keep his secret. Each of them takes a brick, and throws it at the puppet, as they promise not to 'tell'. Everyone watches as the first Friend picks up a brick, and crosses to stand over the puppet.

> What do I say?
> I swear to – (*Stops. Shrugs.*)
> Keep my mouth shut. I promise the others.
> (*Drops brick on puppet.*) I swear to keep my mouth shut. (p. 18)

This is a moment of choice, a 'barrier' moment. Indeed, one of the Friends, Naomi, refuses to take part. The others force a brick into her hand, and drag her over to the puppet. Bond notes:

> This should be painful for us to watch. It demonstrates the barrier that has to be crossed to kill the puppet (or the children). Its (*sic*) part of the play's centre (Bond 2000c).

The groups we worked with recognised that the act of bricking the puppet involves accepting responsibility, making them complicit in Joe's decision to burn down the house. It is this, in part, that makes the 'barrier' difficult to cross. But it is what happens next that provoked the strongest reaction in groups. A boy dies in the fire. When they swore the pact, the Friends did not know this would be the result; so should they feel responsible? Or is Joe the only person to blame? It was *this* question which young people found most troubling. Usman Khalid (Washwood Heath College), for example, thought it was unjust that the Man should seek revenge, not just on Joe, but on his Friends as well: 'They just all said that they would help, but Joe is the one that did it. He should have just killed Joe.' I asked: 'Aren't you all responsible, in a way?' Steph Hegarty said, 'Not really', but Sabida Akhtar (who played Naomi) commented: 'You are.

David Allen

Everyone had something to do with it, 'cos they knew about it. They could have stopped it.'

When, in Scene 5, the Man enters and falls to the ground, the Friends debate what to do with him:

> Can't leave him here.
> He'll be dead in the morning!
> Sod him that's his fault! Leave him!
> Let's go like we said!
> Sod it! Sod it! – a tramp turns up and we're trapped! (pp. 29, 30)

They decide to take him with them as they set out on the journey. This is another 'barrier' moment. It is, perhaps, the critical turning point in the play. In some ways, it may seem to parallel the Palermo improvisation. Their decision to take the Man may appear to contradict our 'common sense' understanding of the world. In fact, cast members frequently questioned if the Friends *would* really do this, in real life. It also led them to consider what *they* would do in this situation. Here, for example, are the reactions of students at Halesowen College:

Faye-Louise Tew: I think they're quite mature – how they are all setting out on a journey and taking care of the man. I mean it's not normal that fourteen-year-old kids would take care of a man. They always seem to make the right decisions.

Russ: If I was in that position, I'd take him.

Laura Richardson: I wouldn't. If a stranger collapsed in front of you, even if you'd done something bad, you wouldn't think, 'Oh, let's take him with us.'

Russ: We're supposed to be little hard knocks, looking after ourselves, number 1. So really, if you wanted us to play that, we wouldn't have picked him up at all.

It is, indeed, a paradox that a group of 'hard knocks' should care for a stranger. Tia Pye (Castle Vale School), however, saw that the Friends, like Joe, switch between caring and destruction – they are 'kind in one scene and fight each other in the next'. Laura Richardson (Halesowen) concluded that the way they care for the Man shows they are not all bad, that they can do good things in their life. Joe's done something bad, and they're all in it with him, but then they kind of turn themselves and help someone. Doing something bad, and doing something good, I know it doesn't mean that you're good, but in a way, if you think about it, it does.

There is, in fact, a simple explanation for why the Friends take the Man with them. In Bond's script, it is indicated that they do not want to be blamed if the man dies.[8] (Nevertheless, we might still feel that, in reality, they would simply run away . . .) In a sense, they are again 'trapped' into responsibility, rather than *choosing* it. They *learn* to care for the Man,

8.   One of the Friends observes that the Man looks dead, and another comments: 'Chriss! – now we'll be blamed for that!' (p. 29).

rather than choosing to care for him. Bond's didactic purpose here is clear: As we have seen, he wants to show that it is only by helping the Man that the Friends 'can become themselves and help each other' (Bond n.d., c).

Bond presents us, then, with an extreme situation. But – unlike the students in the Palermo improvisation – the young people in this drama cannot make their own decision about what to do. They have to take the man with them, because it is in the script. In a sense, they are also trapped into caring. The responsibility is forced on them; they have to learn to care for the Man. In this way, then, the participants in the drama do not choose to take responsibility for 'the world'; rather, looking after the Man seems designed as a form of *preparation* for doing so. It is part of the 'rite of passage'; a way of teaching young people about 'what it is to be human'.

On our first tour of *The Children*, we told groups the story of the play before rehearsals started. For the second tour, we decided only to give a rough outline of the plot, omitting certain key plot developments. Crucially, we did not tell them that the Man they take with them on their journey is going to kill them; we simply talked, vaguely, about the Friends slowly disappearing as the journey progressed – perhaps running away, or going home. We wanted the group to find out gradually what happens, as the audience does. Perhaps this was a bit of a trick to play. However, we felt that if they already know the story in advance, then, in a sense, they cannot take the 'journey' as the characters do. They cannot react to the situations as they occur. The strategy allowed us to discuss the implications of each new event on the journey.

On the first tour, moreover, we discovered a hostility in the attitude of groups to the Man from the start. (One young cast member, for example, insisted he would not take the Man on the journey: 'I'd kill him!') This may have been because they already *knew* the Man was a murderer, and were unable completely to forget that fact. As a result, we were unable to develop much sense of 'caring' in them. We wanted the group to establish their relationship to the Man, *before* they discover he is a murderer.

The moment in the play when the man first kills one of the Friends on stage was always a shock for audiences (who would audibly gasp). This is another 'aggro effect', designed to make us ask 'Why?' Certainly, when we revealed the twist in the story to the cast, it provoked a strong reaction. They had been trapped into caring for the Man; and now they discovered that they were looking after the very thing that was destroying them. Here are some of the comments of students at Egerton Park College:

> I can't believe the man kills the children!!!
> I think the man's personality has completely changed!
> I think it is weird, because in Scene 9 we find out that the man who is supposed to be our friend ends up murdering everyone in the group.

Groups always wanted to talk through the implications of this new development. Why, for example, did the Man choose to kill the Friends first, and save Joe till last? Faye (Halesowen College) observed: 'I think it's because losing his son makes him feel really, really bad, so he wants to get his own back on Joe, before killing him, to make him know what it feels like to lose people close to you.' Kelly Deeley said that he wants Joe to feel responsible: 'It's not just one death now, it's all his friends'.

A question frequently asked at this point was: 'Why does the Man keep-saying, "Good kids. Bless you", if he's killing them?' Young people often saw this as a deliberate deception – 'he's just pretending to like them'. (Emma Burrows at Egerton Park College said: 'I think he says it to make them feel guilty for what they did to his son, he seeks revenge.')

There was a tendency at times to view the behaviour of adults in the play in purely negative terms – to see only the destructiveness, and not the caring. We felt we needed to challenge this. We were able to use the play's dialectic between caring and destruction as a 'learning tool' – to work for what Brecht calls 'complex seeing' (Brecht, 1964: 44). A common view of the mother, for example, was that she has 'a split personality', or even that she is 'a psycho'. When we discussed the issue at Halesowen College, I asked if the mother cares for Joe at all. A number in the group immediately said no; but Kelly said, 'I think she does, in a twisted way.'

Kelly: She's got emotional problems, or she's had some distress . . . Part of her knows that she can walk all over him, but at the same time, she's scared that he's going to leave her. That makes her more angry, so it makes her hit him more.

(This was a perceptive insight. The mother's dependency on Joe explains her feeling of emptiness when he finally leaves her, in Scene Four; she looks around her room and says, 'I have nothing' – p. 26.) In the same group, someone described the man as a 'psycho'. Kelly, however, observed: 'He may have psychological problems, like Joe's mum'.

Loads of people, when something horrible happens in their lives, they tend to react to it, and sometimes they react not in the way they should do . . . I'm not saying loads of people are going to say, 'I'm going to kill you', but people do react like that . . . It's just the way the pain's made them feel.

I read Bond's statement to the group, that the Man and the Mother are destructive 'because they love and need love', and asked: 'Can love make you destructive?'

Kelly: It can, because love's a strong emotion that everyone feels, whether it's for another person, or our family.

Russ: Edward Bond says they need love. They might need love – doesn't mean they're getting it. I mean look at the relationship between Joe and his mother. There's no love there whatsoever . . . She wants love from him, but she ain't going to get it, the way she's acting.

Kelly: I think they do love each other, it's just deep because – she knows she's taking it out on Joe because he's the one there.

Laura: You always take your anger out on the person closest to you.

We discussed the way Joe takes his anger out on the puppet.

Mary Edwards:	I think Joe is doing that because that is what he's shown at home.
Russ:	His mum takes it out on him, but he's got no-one to take it out on, so he takes it out on the puppet.
Terri-Marie Clements-Jones:	The way that the mother looks after the kid could be the same way her mother treated her as a kid. It's a vicious circle.
David:	So how can that circle be broken?
Kelly:	Through Joe learning on his own what love is.

At Castle Vale School, we cast Tia Pye in the role of Jo (played in this case as a girl). Tia saw that Jo switches all the time from loving to violence, because of the way she sees the world around her. Her mother wants love but uses violence to get it. Jo is very much like her mother at the beginning but ends up being the opposite. She changes from a childish girl to an adult, letting go of the past. People of my age [14/15] have to face their demons and grow from them.

Working through objects

Bond argues that once the importance of the 'centre' is understood, 'anything on stage can be used to show it' (Bond 1996a: 168). Indeed, everything 'should be significant – as if it were part of a chinese ideogram' (Bond 2001a: 153).

The Children is full, in fact, of signs that 'point to the play's centre' (Bond 1996a: 145). The contradictions between caring and destruction are given gestic form in the most minute details and actions. So, for example, Joe kills the puppet, and then tries to feed it with some sweets. But the attempt ends in failure; the sweet drops to the ground. Actions such as these are a way of dramatizing care and 'the *absence* of care' (Bond 2000d; italics in original). Bond also makes significant use of objects to point to the play's centre. For example, in Scene 10, the Man cradles a brick as if it is a baby, and then suddenly brings it down on one of the sleeping Friends. The object turns, in an instant, from a baby into murder weapon.

In rehearsal, we were able to explore the meaning of actions and objects. After he has burned down the house, Joe's mother tells him to wash his hands, and then asks: 'Did you hang the towel on the rail?' (p. 20). Later, the Man uses a towel to smother the children, before bricking them. Alicia Hand (Summerhill School, Kingswinford) commented on the paradox that a 'nice, soft, fluffy towel' could be used as a murder weapon.

Bond was once asked if the Man could kill the Friends with a knife, rather than a brick; he refused to countenance this. Alicia saw that a brick is 'ordinary, so you don't expect it to be a murder weapon. Bricks are associated with home, with comfort and security; but here it suggests danger.'

Kate Travers commented: 'You associate bricks with growth, with creativity, with making things. Here, it is used to destroy.'

At one point in Scene 9, one of the Friends hands the Man his towel. Bond comments that we should 'see the towel in isolation. The brick has made us alarmed about objects – the handing of the towel to the man should be disturbing (though done very naturally, of course)' (Bond 2000c). At Summerhill, we explored how the object could be handled in a way that was both natural and disturbing. Kate suggested: 'The Friend should hand the towel as if it is just a towel; but the Man should pause, look at it, and then snatch it suddenly. In his hands, it is no longer a simple towel, it is a murder weapon.' Kate saw, then, that the way the actor uses the object could change its meaning.

In Scene 10, after killing three of the Friends, the Man wipes his face with the towel. We read Bond's description: 'he slowly lifts the murder weapon as if he hasnt [sic] the strength to lift it – its [sic]) just a towel – and then slowly wipes it over his face as he had covered his victims' faces with it' (Bond 2000c). I asked why Bond wanted the action performed so slowly. Kate said: 'Because, as he lifts the towel, it has to turn from murder weapon into a towel again.' We tried the action as Bond described it; it evoked different associations. Some suggested that the Man is washing his face in the blood of his victims. Alicia commented: 'He wants to breathe in the smell of death.' (Similarly, at William Brookes School, Heather Day suggested the Man should hold the towel for a minute, and then suddenly put it on his face, as he does when he is killing the children – suggesting that the Man is also, in a way, killing himself.)

Conclusion

In *The Children*, Bond has created a new form of *Lehrstück*,[9] which is designed to help prepare young people to take 'responsibility for the world'. The play's 'extreme situations' do not function to 'enact' or uncover some quasi-innate sense of our 'shared humanness'. Rather, the play tries to *create* a sense of 'shared humanness' – to teach young people about the need 'to replace revenge with justice, anger with care' (Bond, cited Gold 2000: 10).

At the end of the final MAT tour, one question remained for us: What was the 'centre' of the play, for the young people who performed it? Was it the same as Bond's? Subsequently, several months later, we revisited some of the venues. At each venue, we asked the cast, in groups, to define the centre, as they saw it; and then create a still image of a moment from the play that summed it up for them. What came through strongly in several groups was the idea of loneliness. In William Brookes School, for example, one group chose a moment from the beginning of Scene Six, when a group of Friends are standing, staring into the distance – and wondering why everyone in the world has disappeared. Gabriella Hill commented: 'They are staring into their future – and there's nothing there.' Alicia Hand (Summerhill School) said the play is 'about revenge, because if love can drive you to care, it can

9. Brecht's *Lehrstücke*, or short 'learning plays', were primarily written to be performed by schools' and workers' groups, and choral societies. They were intended to benefit participants more than audiences.

also drive you to kill'. For Kelly Deeley (Halesowen College), the centre is a question: 'a life for a life – can that be right?'. Her group formed an image of the Friends standing round Joe, and Kelly explained: 'Each of them represents a life that gets taken away, torn away from Joe.'

I asked the Halesowen group what Bond means when he states that at the centre of the play is 'the journey to, for humanness'. These are their responses:

Mary:	I think it's 'cos Joe's got a load of weight on his shoulders. He's got loads of responsibility, so he's got to grow up; he's not a child anymore. He takes on the role of an adult.
Faye:	On the journey, they go from children into adults, taking responsibilities, looking after themselves, and looking after a grown man. Maybe it makes them more human.
Kelly:	The journey is for everyone to discover who they are. The choices that they make define who they are, and what they want to be.

I read Bond's statement: 'Children ask the profoundest questions. Children ask: What is justice? Why is our society violent and vengeful?' I wanted to know: 'Have *you* asked those questions?'

Kelly:	I know that I've thought them at some point in my life. The world is screwed up, and the only reason it's screwed up is because loads of people make mistakes, and then loads of people hurt them.
Faye:	People learn from their mistakes.
Kelly:	Not all of them.
David:	The adults in the play don't learn, do they?
Kelly:	The Man's still going to suffer anyway, even though he's killed all of them – 'cos he's going to remember. I know it's 'a life for a life', but how many lives has he killed now?
David:	So revenge doesn't make him happy, then?
Kelly:	Exactly.
Russ:	Where's the justice in that?

Acknowledgements

Gillian Adamson, Claudette Bryanston, Edward Bond, Steph Terpant. The MAT tours of *The Children* in 2004–2005 were funded by Arts Council England. We also received funding from Sir Barry Jackson Trust; Charles Henry Foyle Trust; Bewley Charitable Trust; Bernard Piggot Trust; Bryant Trust; Douglas Turner Trust; Baron Davenport's Charity; Cole Charitable Trust; Keith & Joan Mindelsohn Charitable Trust. For the first tour, the Mother was played by Gina Biggs. For the second tour, the role was played by Sally Williams. The Man was played by Rob Stanley. The Stage Manager was Den Woods.

Works cited

Bas, G. (2005), 'A Glossary of Terms Used in Bondian Theatre' (with Jérôme Hankins), in David Davis (ed.), *Edward Bond and the Dramatic Child*, Stoke-on-Trent: Trentham Books, pp. 201–220.

Bond, E. (1993), *Olly's Prison*, London: Methuen.

—— (1994), 'Tonbandprotokoll eines Gesprächs mit Edward Bond', Discussion between Edward Bond, Peter Palitzsch, Karl Kneidl and Stephan Wetzel, Cambridge, England, 18 February 1994. Preserved in the archive of the Berliner Ensemble. (Quoted with permission.)

—— (1995), *Edward Bond, Letters II*, in Ian Stuart (ed.), Luxembourg: Harwood Academic Publishers.

—— (1996a), *Edward Bond, Letters III*, in Ian Stuart (ed.), Amsterdam: Harwood Academic Publishers.

—— (1996b), 'Rough Notes on Theatre', *SCYPT Journal*, 31, pp. 8–17.

—— (1998a), 'Commentary on *The War Plays*', in *Bond Plays 6*, London: Methuen.

—— (1998b), *Red, Black and Ignorant*, in *Plays 6*, London: Methuen.

—— (1998c), *Edward Bond, Letters 4*, in Ian Stuart (ed.), Amsterdam: Harwood Academic Publishers.

—— (2000a), 'Words about *The Children*', in the programme for the original Classworks Theatre production.

—— (2000b), Unpublished letter to Claudette Bryanston, 16 January 2000.

—— (2000c), 'Notes on *The Children*', unpublished letter to Classworks Theatre Company, 12 February 2000.

—— (2000d), Unpublished letter to Classworks Theatre Company, 26 February 2000.

—— (2000e), *The Children & Have I None*, London: Methuen.

—— (2000f), *The Hidden Plot: Notes on Theatre and the State*, London: Methuen.

—— (2001a), *Edward Bond, Letters 5*, Ian Stuart (ed.), London: Routledge.

—— (2001b), 'En situation extreme, je prononce mon commencement', *Mouvement*, 11, pp. 40–49.

—— (2001c), 'Le sens du désastre', *Registres (Revue d'études théâtrales)*, 6, pp. 137–147.

—— (2002), Transcript of keynote speech at a seminar on 'The Quality of Children's Theatre', organised by Arts Council England, and held in Birmingham, 9 July 2002. http://www.artscouncil.org.uk/documents/publications.704.doc. Accessed 19 August 2006.

—— (2003a), *The Cap*, in *Plays 7*, London: Methuen.

—— (2003b), 'Questions from *Theater der Zeit* concerning *Die Kinder*', unpublished paper dated 12 January 2003. (This paper was subsequently used as the basis of a piece by Thomas Irmer, 'Menschen müssen nicht destruktiv sein', in *Theater der Zeit*, February 2003, pp. 56, 57.)

—— (2003c), Unpublished letter to the author, 27 December 2003.

—— (2003d), Unpublished talk given at Newman College, Birmingham, 12 October 2003.

—— (2004a), 'Modern drama and the invisible object', *The Journal for Drama in Education*, 20: 2, pp. 24–32.

—— (2004b), Unpublished letter to the author, 11 October 2004.

—— (2004c), Unpublished letter to the author, 18 December 2004.

—— (2004d), 'Le problème d'être humain' (interview with Laurence Cazaux and Thierry Guichard), *Le matricule des anges*, 49, pp. 18–23.

—— (2005a), 'Something of Myself', in David Davis (ed.), *Edward Bond and the Dramatic Child*, Stoke-on-Trent: Trentham Books, pp. 1–8.

———— (2005b), 'Drama Devices', in David Davis (ed.), ibid., pp. 84–92.

———— (2005c), Unpublished letter to Robert Woodruff, 19 January 2005.

———— (2006), 'Pour les jeunes acteurs qui jouent *Les Enfants* à Beyrouth', in B. Chauvet, É. Duchâtel, E. Bond, J. Hankins and D. Tuaillon (eds.), *Pièces de guerre I et II*, Paris: CNDP, p. 127.

———— (n.d., a), 'Density (Notes on Drama and the Logic of Imagination)', (unpublished paper).

———— (n.d., b), Unpublished letter to Bill Roper.

———— (n.d., c), Unpublished letter to Sorrell Oates and Matt Morris-Jones.

———— (n.d., d), 'The Prisoner's Site' (unpublished paper). (An abridged version of this paper was published as 'Something of myself': see 2005a, above.)

Brecht, B. (1964), *Brecht on Theatre*, translated by John Willett, London: Methuen.

Doona, J. (2005), 'The sheet of glass', in David Davis (ed.), *Edward Bond and the Dramatic Child*, Stoke-on-Trent: Trentham Books, pp. 93–110.

Duchâtel, Éric (2006), '*Les Enfants*', in B. Chauvet, É. Duchâtel, E. Bond, J. Hankins and D. Tuaillon, *Pièces de guerre I et II*, Paris: CNDP, pp. 124–127.

Gold, K. (2000), 'Children Know the World is Violent and Vengeful', *Times Educational Supplement*, 18 February 2000, pp. 8–10.

Innes, C. (1982), 'The Political Spectrum of Edward Bond: From Rationalism to Rhapsody', *Modern Drama*, 25: 2, pp. 189–206.

Palitzsch, P. (1994), 'Tonbandprotokoll eines Gesprächs mit Edward Bond' (see Bond 1994, above).

Singer, A. (2000), 'Improvised Insight into Grown-Up World', *Cambridge Evening News*, 24 February. (Photocopy of article supplied by Classworks Theatre Company. No page number preserved on copy.)

Sophocles (1994), *Plays: One*, London: Methuen.

Stuart, I. (1994), 'Interview with Edward Bond', *Journal of Dramatic Theory and Criticism*, 8: 2, pp. 129–146.

———— (ed.) (2001), *Selections from the Notebooks of Edward Bond*, Vol. 2, 1980–1995, London: Methuen.

Suggested citation

Allen, D. (2007), '"Going to the Centre": Edward Bond's *The Children*', *Studies in Theatre and Performance* 27: 2, pp. 115–136, doi: 10.1386/stap.27.2.115/1

Contributor details

David Allen is currently artistic director of the Midland Actors Theatre (MAT). He is the author of *Stanislavsky for Beginners* (1999) and *Performing Chekhov* (Routledge 2000), as well as several articles on Bond's work, including 'Between Brecht and Bond' in the *Brecht Yearbook* (Summer 2005). He directed Bond's *The Children* for MAT in 2004–2005.
E-mail: news@midlandactorstheatre.co.uk

Studies in Theatre and Performance Volume 27 Number 2 © 2007 Intellect Ltd
Article. English language. doi: 10.1386/stap.27.2.137/1

Singular impressions: Meta-theatre on Renaissance celebrities and corpses

Jenn Stephenson

Abstract

Theatrical corpses and celebrities never fail to evoke a peculiar awareness of the performative nature of the play as a real-world event for the audience, and so both corpses and celebrities are always meta-theatrical. By applying a phenomenological model in order to separate staged objects into their dual components of actual and fictional noemata (virtual sense impressions), it becomes clear that these particular objects – celebrities and corpses – create a unique kind of meta-theatre, replacing the typical perceptual ambiguous duality of the fictional and the actual with an obstinately singular impression of the actual. Renaissance plays provide a rich and sophisticated field of examples wherein the plays pick up this essential meta-theatricality and construct second-level self-reflexive comments, playing variations on this basic perceptual problem. Ultimately, this analysis proposes a model that might profitably be applied to other instances of meta-theatre that present only a single actual noema, such as self-reflexive references to space and time.

Keywords

Renaissance English
  drama

meta-theatre

phenomenology

audience

corpses

celebrities

In the summer of 2002, I saw *Richard III* at the Stratford Festival (Stratford, Ontario, Canada) with Tom McCamus in the title role. As so often happens with well-known actors, especially those who appear regularly with a single company, and even more especially with a repertory company like the one at Stratford, my experience of McCamus as Richard was haunted by the ghosts of characters past; characters from years ago and characters from yesterday's matinée – the residuum of my own theatregoing history at this particular theatre: McCamus as Horner in *The Country Wife*, as Edmund in *Long Day's Journey into Night*, as Vladimir in *Waiting for Godot*. (I didn't see *The Threepenny Opera* and so missed McCamus as Macheath). To each audience member, the actor's body becomes a variable palimpsest where new characters overwrite old characters, but never completely efface them. Caught up in the drama of *Richard III*, my primary impression was that of Richard Duke of Gloucester, but a familiar gesture or intonation could unexpectedly bring forth any of these others. This is the effect of celebrity. In *The Haunted Stage*, Marvin Carlson treats this resonant colliding experience of the dramatic past and present and identifies the actor in general and celebrity in particular as being a potent site for ghosting.[1] But this kind of ghosting need not be limited to a specific previous playgoing experience. It can also extend to the conventions of playgoing in general, highlighting what or who the actor is as well as what or who he is not.

1. 'The most familiar example of this phenomenon is the appearance of an actor, remembered from previous roles, in a new characterization. The recycled body of an actor, already a complex bearer of semiotic messages, will almost inevitably in a new role evoke the ghost or ghosts of previous roles . . . a phenomenon that often colours and indeed may dominate the reception process' (8). Regarding celebrity Carlson writes 'But even when an actor strives to vary his roles, he is, especially as his reputation grows, entrapped by the memories of his public, so that each

new appearance requires a renegotiation with those memories' (9).

2. All quotations from Shakespeare's plays are taken from *The Riverside Shakespeare*, 2nd edn. (ed. by G. Blakemore Evans), Boston: Houghton Mifflin, 1997. Spelling has been regularised where necessary and editorial marks have been removed.

3. The theatrical effect 'refers to stage action that immediately reveals its playful, artificial and theatrical origins . . . It reminds the audience of its spectator status by bringing out the theatricality or theatricalisation of the stage', Patrice Pavis, *Dictionary of the Theatre: Terms, Concepts and Analysis*, trans. by Christine Shantz, Toronto: University of Toronto Press, 1998, p. 394.

Also in the same production, a very demanding athletic combat was staged between Richard and Richmond (Graham Abbey). Richmond killed Richard. Then Abbey stood over the body and proclaimed 'God and your arms be prais'd, victorious friends, The day is ours, the bloody dog is dead' (5.5.1–2) while McCamus lay on the stage still quite obviously breathing heavily from the exertion of the fight. This is one of the most extreme examples I have witnessed of the irreconcilably breathing corpse. The primary impression again may be Richard dead, but faced with conflicting evidence, the audience must process competing impressions of the dead character and the living actor both occupying the same moment in time and space. This is the effect of staged corpses.

Theatrical corpses and celebrities never fail to evoke a peculiar awareness of the performative in the audience. I will argue that this performative awareness stems from strong outside knowledge of the actual, which compels recognition of the irreconcilable ontological divide between the fictional and actual. In this way, the staging of corpses and celebrities is always meta-theatrical. Awareness of the actual in competition with the fictional reminds the audience once again that this is a play and so operates to offer a 'meta' comment on its theatricality. The aim of this paper is twofold. First, it will describe how, in phenomenological terms, the staging of celebrities and corpses functions as meta-theatre in precisely the same way, both presenting aggressively singular impressions that unbalance the typical duality of aesthetic experience. And second, by unpacking this atypical meta-theatrical strategy, to demonstrate the general effects of second-order meta-theatre, which comments on theatrical perception by showing breakdowns of that perception.

A confluence of historical performance conditions on the early modern English stage, including daylight performance, the bare minimally adorned stage and boy-players in female parts, demanded significant interpretive work on the part of the audience to manage the relationship between the actual – day, stage, boy – and the fictional – night, world, woman. Subject to such conditions, the perceptual gap between the fictional and the actual is wide and inescapable. Witness the opening exchange between sentinels Barnardo and Francisco: 'Tis now struck twelve. Get thee to bed, Francisco.' 'For this relief much thanks. 'Tis bitter cold, And I am sick at heart' (*Hamlet* 1.1.7–8).[2] For an audience present to a mild weather, day-lit performance, the theatrical effect is palpable.[3] The audience must work to transpose their actual surroundings to that of the fictional world into which they are being invited. The chorus in *Henry V* reflects on this perceptual effort: 'Think when we talk of horses, that you see them/Printing their proud hoofs i' th' receiving earth;/For 'tis your thoughts that now must deck our kings' (Prologue 26–28). Many Renaissance plays adopt this strategy. They identify perceptual gaps of this kind between the real world and the represented world and then build on this basic situation to comment on the process whereby audiences work to reconcile these opposing poles, attempting to close or at least minimize the stress of the perceptual gap.

The manifested tension between the two poles of the actual and the fictional generates a primary strongly self-aware theatrical effect and also produces opportunities for secondary self-reflexive commentary on that effect.

Among phenomenological critics considering the engagement of the perceiving audience-subject with art, both Bert O. States and Mikel Dufrenne examine this observed tension between the actual and the fictional at play in aesthetic representation. In his *Phenomenology of the Aesthetic Experience*, Mikel Dufrenne separates the art object into two components; the work of art and the aesthetic object (Dufrenne: 3). As a work of art, the art object is described in its physical being. To this view, a painting consists of canvas, frame and paint. The sculpture is stone or wood or metal. In the theatre, this aspect of the performance encompasses the actor as actor, the stage as stage and the sets and costumes as constructed from wood, paper and fabric. As an aesthetic object, the art object is transformed. A painting becomes a bowl of fruit or a nude reclining; the sculpture a bird in flight; and the actor becomes Hamlet, the stage the court at Elsinore. Both these aspects of the art object exist simultaneously, housed in the same physical entity, and constituting an innate duality in every art object between the actual (the work of art) and the fictional (the aesthetic object). In phenomenological terms, following Edmund Husserl, each of these perceived aspects of the same object presents a different virtual sense impression or *noema* – the actual noema of the actor, for example, and the fictional noema of the character. The key to distinguishing the actor noema from the character noema lies in the perceiving attitude or *noesis* that is brought to bear on the impressions given. Dufrenne's work of art manifests through the natural or positing attitude, which privileges the actual noema. Whereas the noesis of audiencing privileges the fictional noema, and the art object manifests to consciousness in Dufrenne's terms as an aesthetic object.[4] Oscillating between these two perspectives, both noemata always remain, however one is temporarily displaced by the other. The displaced noema is, in phenomenological terms, deemed to be absent but co-present or co-intended.

Having placed the responsibility for the identification of an aesthetic object with the perceiving audience, and having laid out the innate duality of works of art, which always manifest both actual and fictional faces, Dufrenne does not go on to discuss meta-theatre or the potential for self-referentiality as a result of the duality of theatrical objects. However, he does consider the appropriate balance of belief concerning the relative reality of the two noemata required for an audience and identifies the inter-dependent relation between the fictional noema positioned out front and the actual noema standing behind. Describing his own audiencing experience, he writes,

> I indeed relate to Tristan and Isolde through the singers, but not as a dupe. I do not call a doctor when I see Tristan stretched out on his couch, and I am fully aware that he is a legendary being who is as mythical as a centaur. Besides, marginal perceptions keep reminding me that I am at the theatre as

4. English lacks an appropriate word to describe the particular cognitive experience of attending a play. (French uses the verb *s'assister*, which points to active generative work being done by the audience to make the play). Spectators merely see. Playgoers go to a play but this term doesn't indicate what they do once there. Audiences do more than their etymological root of simply hearing (*audire*) indicates. And so audiencing is a word of my own coinage to fill this terminological gap.

In contrast to Dufrenne's coolly balanced state, we see a fictional example of inappropriate audience stance in the person of the Grocer's Wife in Beaumont's *The Knight of the Burning Pestle*. This lady, witness to a play, is concerned for the safety of the characters. In Act 3, when Jasper draws his sword and threatens to kill Luce, the Wife urges her husband to 'raise the watch at Ludgate and bring a *mittimus* from the justice for this desperate villain' (3.92–93). Inside the provisional reality of the London of 'The London Merchant' (the 'real' play within the play), the power of the watch and the justice's warrant is of course void. Likewise, actual-world money is introduced to pay a fictional-world debt. After Rafe spends the night at an inn, the Host threatens to seize him for non-payment of his bill. From the audience, the Wife urges her husband to pay the Host the twelve shillings owed (3.174–178). Our amusement at the antics of this character originates in our awareness of her behaviour as foolhardy and inappropriate.

a spectator . . . I accept without difficulty such unlikely things as, for example, that the dying Tristan has so much voice left for singing. (Dufrenne: 9)

Here, Dufrenne as an operagoer deliberately limits his belief in the fictional noema as real. As he says, he is not a dupe and does not call a doctor for the dying Tristan. Belief in the character's reality status is limited by what Dufrenne terms marginal impressions. These impressions are founded on incursions into the foreground of perception by actual noemata. In this case, impressions are dependent on the awareness of Tristan as a trained singer. Under this audiencing strategy, Dufrenne manages to keep the fictional noema in check by permitting some small awareness too of the actual noema. As Dufrenne's translator Edward S. Casey notes, this act of balancing competing noemata echoes Coleridge's call for a 'willing suspension of disbelief' (Casey: xviii). Contrary to the ordinary employment of this quotation, Coleridge does not, in fact, advocate a complete surrender to the proposed reality of a fictional world. Rather he posits a somewhat cooler attitude that accounts for the fictional by reference to the actual: 'The true stage-illusion in this and in all other things consists – not in the mind's judging it to be a forest, but, in its remission of the judgement that it is not a forest' (Coleridge: 4.37). In this remission of judgement, in the studied refusal to decide, the audience deliberately chooses not to expose the reality behind the fictional forest. And in this negative belief there is an implied awareness of the actual noema that is not a forest. This ambivalent, balanced stance is the typical 'correct' audiencing stance. The fictional noema is provisionally privileged as 'real' but the actual noema remains to remind us that the events on the stage are not in fact real and do not require a real world audience response as Dufrenne rightly notes.[5]

Dufrenne identifies the source of his somewhat detached stance from the dying Tristan as 'marginal impressions'. He writes, 'Attention turns away from what is marginal so as not to take it [the fictional reality] too seriously. I accord it only a potential rather than an actual existence, a neutral one in any case, unless an incident such as a loud-talking neighbour or a power failure leads me back into what Husserl calls a positing attitude' (Dufrenne: 7). For Dufrenne, marginal impressions are key to the maintenance of the ambivalent belief stance. However, impressions like the loud-talking neighbour exceed the marginal and disrupt the careful balance. These intrusive impressions insist on the replacement of the fictional noema with the actual; the actual comes to the fore and the fictional is set aside as co-intended. Disruptions of the kind that Dufrenne lists relate to the actual experience of playgoing. Coughing, rumbling traffic outside the theatre and an unexpected power-cut all exist beyond the scope of the fictional. It is true that these disruptions do create a perceptual shift to the natural or positing attitude, the same kind of shift instigated by meta-theatre. But since these disruptions are not themselves theatrical they don't count as meta-theatre proper, but Dufrenne is certainly moving in that direction. This now brings our attention around to those actualising impressions that emanate from the qualities of the stage instead of from the house. When stage elements themselves move to disrupt the fictional and promote the actual, we get meta-theatre. By drawing excessive attention to the actual underpinnings of theatrical structures and conventions, meta-theatre reverses Dufrenne's normative audiencing process of neutralization. Impressions that are more than marginal are no longer just helpfully neutral to the fictional reality but are actually destructive.

'If you know not me': Meta-theatre and celebrity

One such actual impression that jeopardises the security of the fictional reality is that of the celebrity actor. Normally, the actor's body is subject to what I term the embodiment–effacement convention. Under this theatrical perceptual practice, the actual noema of the actor is phenomenologically transposed by the audience into the fictional noema of the character. We accept that Richard Burbage becomes Hamlet. We then place Hamlet at the forefront of our perception and relegate Burbage to the status of absent but co-intended. The fictional character is successfully embodied and the actual actor is effectively effaced. In the case of celebrity, the transposition process is placed under stress as the audience attempts to properly transpose this actual person into his proper fictional existence. But, the problem of the actual celebrity noema lies with having encountered something too real. The result of this encounter is often a failed embodiment because of the failed effacement of self. For a famous actor, the audience's awareness of his or her actual-world self is too strong and is not easily supplanted by the character persona.[6] Carlson categorises this actual-world reference to the actor's life outside the theatre as another source of ghosting: 'This is the haunting of a new interpretation by the audience's knowledge of or assumptions about the actor's life outside the theatre' (Carlson: 85). I would suggest that this perceptual ghosting stemming from an acute awareness of the actual is not limited to knowledge or even speculation about the details of a celebrity actor's life *per se*, but extends from the simple identification of that person as a celebrity, that is, as a strongly defined real-world figure. It is this ineffaceable quality of the self that makes dramatic celebrities necessarily meta-theatrical at the primary level simply by their appearance on the stage.[7] And this virtually inescapable disruption of the fictional in favour of the actual makes celebrity an attractive target for self-aware second-order commentary.

This attraction to the phenomenon of the stubbornly actual actor noema ascendant over its fictional counterpart can be seen in a handful of plays from the early modern period, where the casting of celebrities becomes fodder for playful commentary. In *Greene's Tu Quoque*, a piece of comic business depends on this meta-theatrical power of celebrity to displace or at least resonate with the character. Here, the player Thomas Greene in the character of Bubble debates going to a play:

Geraldine: Why then we'll go to the Red Bull; they say Greene's a good clown.
Bubble: Greene? Greene's an Ass.

6. This is especially true in Hollywood films when big-name stars play roles where the character's name is of little importance. Apart from eponymous roles, ask yourself if you can remember the names of any characters played by Julia Roberts or Tom Hanks.

7. In 'Celebrity and the semiotics of acting' (*New Theatre Quarterly*, 6:22 (1990), 154–161), Michael L. Quinn observes that 'this relatively direct exchange of expressive signs and outside knowledge splits the acting sign much like the sign is split by Brecht in his verfremdungseffekt' (156). Although he takes a semiotic approach rather than the phenomenological approach that I am following here, Quinn identifies the same difficulty between the personal expressive function of acting, which comes to the foreground and so overpowers the referential function of the stage figure.

Scattergood:	Wherefore do you say so?
Bubble:	Indeed I have no reason: for they say, he is as like me as ever he can look. (1571–1576)

Another variation on this meta-theatrical play features in the induction to Marston's *The Malcontent*. Under circumstances that are not entirely clear, ownership of the playscript for *The Malcontent* was transferred from the Children of the Queen's Revels at Blackfriars to the King's Men. When it was performed at the Globe, an induction by John Webster was added. In this new opening scene, the actor William Sly enters playing a member of the audience who seats himself on the stage. He then demands to speak to some of the actors of the company, naming particularly Henry Condell, Richard Burbage and himself, William Sly. Three actors come out to speak with him; and they are Burbage, Condell and a third man John Lowin. Sly interrogates them concerning the play's transfer to the King's Men. Finally, Sly offers a silly prologue and then, presumably, they all exit – there is no indication in the text that Sly remains onstage through the main action of the play. After the appearance of the three actors, none of the performers takes any notice that Lowin is not Sly, and the self-requesting paradox dissipates. In both examples above, the meta-theatrical turn depends on the audience's correct identification of Bubble as Greene and of the intrusive audience member as the actor William Sly. Both examples position a fictional character to comment on the actual characteristics of the effaced actor and so speak against himself. Through this device, attention is drawn to the overcharged dual noematic status of the actor and character both housed in one body. In the induction to *The Malcontent*, the awareness of this duality is augmented as there is an additional moment of curiosity as the audience wonders how the problem of Sly paradoxically demanding to see himself will be solved. (For Greene to encounter himself in the parallel example, the characters would in fact need to go to the Red Bull and see Greene there. While the characters do not then go to the Red Bull, paradoxically, they are in fact already there, since the Red Bull was the home of Queen Anne's Men at the time of the play and was almost certainly the actual world performance venue.) Here, Sly is ontologically divided against himself and the two noematic selves cannot meet. By making this impossible request, the actor Sly calls into question the relationship of the competing noemata. The ontological status of Burbage and the other actors who enter the scene supposedly 'as themselves' is contrasted with that of Sly 'as audience' who is one fictional level removed from the actual self that he demands to see.

In a slightly more involved scenario, akin to my initial example of the actor as palimpsest concerning Tom McCamus as *Richard III* and others, Andrew Gurr suggests another potential instance of meta-theatre of the celebrity convention in the casting of *Julius Caesar* and *Hamlet*. When Polonius claims to have previously played Caesar at university and been 'kill'd i' th' Capitol' (*Hamlet* 3.2.103–104), Gurr imagines a knowing wink when the actor playing Caesar (possibly John Heminges), having been killed by Brutus (possibly Richard Burbage), is again killed as Polonius by the same actor now playing Hamlet (Gurr, *Playgoing*: 106). This meta-theatrical moment, like those described in *Greene's Tu Quoque* and *The Malcontent*, is not a pure example, however, because the perceptual oscillation required to make this self-referral work, which depends on the shift to the audience's recognition of the actors as actors, is only half the equation since the allusory external knowledge of the casting in the earlier play is also needed. To complete the circuit, the audience needs to reach out of the fictional world and draw on a specific actual world experience. Whereas in the first two plays mentioned there is a single connection between one actor and one character, Gurr's *Hamlet*/*Julius Caesar* reference forms a double connection linking two characters from two different fictional worlds via the bridge of the actual actor and the audience's actual-world experience of attending plays; here specifically two productions – first the Chamberlain's Men's *Julius Caesar* and then their *Hamlet*. But it is also possible to generate this triangular bridged relationship between an actual noema and two fictional noemata within a single play, thus eliminating the need for outside knowledge. The way to do this is through transparent doubling.

Richard Tarlton, in a performance of *The Famous Victories of Henry the Fifth*, made good use of the meta-theatrical bridging afforded to celebrities to draw a laugh. As re-counted in *Tarlton's Jests*, the actor playing the judge was for some reason absent and Tarlton stepped into the role in addition to his normal role as the clown. As the judge Tarlton received a box on the ear from Prince Henry. After the judge exited, Tarlton returned immediately as the clown and inquired of the other actors what had transpired:

> O, saith one, hadst thou been here thou shouldest have seen Prince Henry hit the Judge a terrible box on the ear. What man, said Tarlton, strike a Judge. It is true, saith the other. No other like, saith Tarlton, and it could not but be terrible to the Judge when it so terrifies me, that methinks the blow remains still on my cheek, that it burns again. The people laughed at this mightily.[8]

Again, two fictional characters are perceptually linked through the actual status of the celebrity actor. However, meta-theatrical resonance in this case relies less on the fame of the particular actor than on the marked reaction to the blow that has affected two different characters in one actor body. The single body takes the blow and it is felt by both occupant characters. The traditional separation between doubled characters is breached by Tarlton as the clown in his verbal acceptance of the shared physical experience (and perhaps visually by a red cheek). The simple recognition of one actor in two roles functions in a simple meta-theatrical mode to remind the audience of the absent but co-present actor noema. But, Shakespeare as interpreted by Gurr and Tarlton shows that this simple awareness at the heart of the embodiment-effacement convention can itself be fodder for self-referential commentary and so create secondary

8. Richard Tarlton, *Tarlton's Jests* (London, 1638) sig. C3. This anecdote first came to my attention in Sally-Beth MacLean and Scott McMillin, *The Queen's Men and Their Plays*, Cambridge: Cambridge UP, 1998, p. 89.

9. This metatheatre of celebrity casting is pointed up in the movie *Working Girl* (1988) when Sigourney Weaver's character returns from a skiing holiday carrying an oversize stuffed toy gorilla, certainly a sly reference to her previous film *Gorillas in the Mist* (1988).

meta-theatre on that basic awareness. It is clear from the Tarlton jest that, although celebrity is helpful in bridging two fictional characters to engender a meta-theatrical awareness of theatre as theatre, the central requirement is merely audience identification of a specific actor-character correlation. Of course, fame facilitates this identification, but that awareness can be generated in a more overt fashion by what the characters say about their previous intradramatic incarnations.

It is accepted that doubling played a role in the plays of the Tudor and Stuart public stages. However, there is no consensus among scholars of the era about how this practice operated, whether or not playwrights deliberately plotted doubled pairs, and whether or not audiences drew the pleasure of recognition from identifying them. Nevertheless, there are moments where at least the potential for meta-theatrical commentary and awareness do break through, whether or not they are intentional and without the historical supporting evidence for an audience reaction, unlike Tarlton's note: 'The people laughed mightily.' One of these moments arises in *Richard II* Act 4 Scene 1 regarding the quarrel between Aumerle and Fitzwater. The resolution of their disagreement depends on the testimony of the banished Norfolk. Bolingbroke declares that 'These differences shall rest under gage/Till Norfolk be repeal'd. Repeal'd he shall be' (4.1.86–87). The Bishop of Carlisle, a bystander to this scene, seizes this opportunity to deliver the news that Norfolk cannot be repealed because he has since died in Venice. Alan Armstrong argues that this piece of dialogue is moving toward a pointed meta-theatrical joke, if the Bishop of Carlisle is Norfolk. That is, if the same actor who played Norfolk banished in 1.3 returns to play Carlisle in 4.1. The character cannot be repealed not only because he died a fictional death in Venice, but also because the actor whose body he occupied has moved on to play another character. When the audience 'sees' Norfolk standing before them, the character is simultaneously dead in spirit but paradoxically resurrected to some extent in body. The seemingly redundant lines that follow the revelation of Norfolk's death seem to point explicitly to this exchange:

Bolingbroke: Why, Bishop is Norfolk dead?
Carlisle: As surely as I live, my lord. (*Richard II* 4.1.101–102)

Both Bolingbroke's question and Carlisle's response yoke together Norfolk and the Bishop. Carlisle in particular associates the dead Norfolk with his own living corporeal presence as Carlisle. Success for this kind of meta-theatrical turn is dependent on the audience recognising the same actor in both roles. And so the direct articulation of the doubling at work creates a kind of 'local' celebrity, making the actor playing Norfolk/Carlisle known to the audience even if we don't know his name.

Celebrities, who remain resolutely actual, manifest the clearest appearances of the actor as palimpsest haunted by faint traces of previous roles and also occasionally by details of the actor's real life.[9] This is true of all actors, but typically it is suppressed by the persuasive impression of the character noema. The disruptive awareness of this actorly characteristic of embodiment residue surfaces to perception in the case of famous actors or when the performer is known personally to the audience, or when he is made known to the audience through an explicit reference to prior roles. In every case of celebrity-based meta-theatre, the fictional-world noema is persistently overwhelmed by the insistent phenomenal impression of the actor as a person. Whereas the ambivalent belief stance described by Dufrenne and Coleridge permits oscillation or ambiguity between the competing noemata, disruption of this balance by a strongly actual impression eliminates the normal ambiguous duality of staged objects, renders the manifestation of the fictional noema particularly difficult and leaves only the single noema of the actual. The aggressively singular impression created by celebrities and commented on by meta-theatre is a factor of the distance between the paired noemata. The identification of the actor as actor compels the audience to consider how unlike the character he is. It is that distance that instigates the meta-theatrical double vision, emphasising the irreconcilability of the two halves.

Turning to Bert O. States' *Great Reckonings in Little Rooms*,[10] States, like Dufrenne, discusses the innate phenomenological duplexity of staged objects without delving into the self-referential fallout that I argue necessarily follows from the awareness of this duplexity. States targets theatrical events of the destructive kind that I am imagining where the actual breaks through the façade of the fictional. To illustrate these 'upsurges of the real', he selects, as his basic example of theatrically challenging elements, objects that possess a high degree of iconicity – objects that obdurately remain themselves within the fictional context (States: 34). In contrast to the example of celebrities where the distance between the actual actor and the fictional character that she aims to embody is so great that it is difficult to perceptually overcome, these self-identical objects are so close to their fictional counterparts that the same meta-theatrical effect of aggressive noematic singularity is triggered. Standing firm against their integration into the fictional world, objects with this ability resist the transposition to stage objects. States include in the list of these stubbornly actual objects ticking clocks, animals on the stage, running water, live flame and child actors (States: 30–34). Any object or occurrence that is blatantly real fails to be sufficiently integrated into the fictional world and operates in such a way as to distract the audience from the reality effect, pointing up the fact that the spectacle witnessed is artificial. Working backward through the attempted transposition, the audience retraces the path whereby these real objects have been brought to the stage. Instead of allowing the objects to be passively absorbed by them into the fictional world, the audience is more interested in their real-world status. Located at the extreme end of the perceptual spectrum, these objects are so attached to the real world that the transposition process required to absorb them into the fictional world is unusually difficult. The effect of this resistance is that when

10. The subtitle of States's book is 'On the Phenomenology of Theater', but he himself acknowledges in his introduction that what he offers 'is not even a phenomenology of the theater, properly speaking' (1). The descriptions that he provides are only phenomenological in the vague sense that they awaken 'the reader's memory of his own perceptual encounters with theater (1). For a more detailed critique of States's use of phenomenology, see Craig Stewart Walker, 'Reckoning with States on the phenomenology of theatre', *Journal of Dramatic Theory and Criticism*, 11:2 (1997), pp. 65–83.

11. A theatre company in the UK called 1157 performancegroup made news in the spring of 2004 with a casting call for a corpse. The group is preparing a play called *Dead . . . you will be*, which proposes to examine the social taboos surrounding death. The performance was initially scheduled for May 2004 but has since been indefinitely postponed. It is not clear to what extent the staged corpse will be fictionalised.

placed on the stage objects of this type retain their real-world status and disturb the reality effect built up by the remainder of the stage image. As unsuccessfully transposed objects, they trigger a reminder for the audience that the entire play is an artificial product of the transposition process. And as such these objects perform as meta-theatre, displacing the fictional world and foregrounding the actual theatrical situation. But this situation is not restricted to the particular objects with which States are occupied.

'Now am I dead': Meta-theatre and corpses

A corpse on the stage is exactly a States-type object. The problem of the proximate relationship between the fictional correlative of unreflected audiencing and the real-world correlative brought to the surface by the meta-theatrical noesis finds its terminal example in dramatic deaths. However, the case for corpses is a little different from that of celebrity. Whereas it is awareness of the actual celebrity actor that causes the disruption of the fictional world, an actual corpse is impossible. The actual taking of a life and subsequently the staging of a corpse remains a theatrical taboo.[11] Some of States's obstinate objects are also subject to theatrical taboo in a small way. Live animals and live flames, as well as objects that States do not include but which function in a similar way, like real alcohol and real money, generate perceptual discomfort because they create risk on the stage. The actual-world capacities of these objects for unpredictable behaviour – fire, drunkenness and theft – get in the way of their fictional assimilation. Later on, I will talk more about meta-theatre and fear of the too-real. But for the moment, the corpse stands in this company as an object that is not desirable on the stage. Like these other objects, it would be, one imagines, too real and as such quite worrisome. The actual and the fictional in this case are not too distant and therefore irreconcilable as celebrities are, but in fact too close, being identical and so irreconcilable. An audience may accept an actual chair in the role of fictional chair, but an actual corpse makes us uncomfortable. But, surprisingly perhaps, the performance of a fictional corpse triggers the same perceptual discomfort because it is so strong, strong in a similar manner to the celebrity. And like celebrity, the perceptual distance between the fictional noema of the dead body and the actual noema of the living actor playing dead is immense.

A corollary to the basic embodiment–effacement convention is the rule that there are limits to the extent of the embodiment of which the actor is capable. As a perceptual phenomenon, the character is often granted abilities that are beyond the representational power of the actor. This limitation of the actor occurs because in addition to the noema of the actor as actor, the actor is also a real-world object, which has been bracketed from consideration as part of the process of theatrical reception. So although the actor as object has been perceptually set aside, the confining body of the actor cannot be fully shed. On the other hand, the character is noema only, the result of a noetic act of imagination without a real-world counterpart. And so there are objects and actions that, when portrayed on the stage, are not possible (or extraordinarily unlikely) or not desirable that they be identical to the equivalent real-world actions or objects. Death is the ultimate example of failed embodiment. When a character dies, the audience can be within a hair's breadth of absolute certainty that the actor portraying that character is not truly dead, that in fact she is only feigning.[12]

Ordinary death or serious injury is a staple of the drama. Hamlet and Laertes are both killed in their exhibition duel before the court; Othello smothers Desdemona; Romeo drinks poison. In *The Spanish Tragedy*, Hieronimo memorably bites out his own tongue. All in full view of the audience. Regarding dramatic representation, there are levels of fidelity and the audience is preternaturally flexible concerning what it accepts as convincing – or at least not disrupting. A stage kiss is a real kiss. A stage slap is often a real slap but sometimes not. A stage death is certainly (hopefully) not a real death. Audiences are not positioned so as to distinguish between the perception of another's real pain and feigned pain, but audiences can be (mostly) certain to distinguish between feigned death or serious injury and the real thing. According to the dictates of convention, when a character dies, the actor is not also dead. With this certainty in place, even the basic case of a simple unreflected death becomes meta-theatrical at the primary level because the audience knows that the actor is not really dead. As when presented with the unaffected child actor or the oblivious dog on the stage wagging its tail, the audience is impressed with how well death is acted. When presented with a corpse, we check for breathing.[13] Death is always meta-theatrical.[14] The discrepancy of the dual view presented by the breathing corpse arises because in death the actor attempts the embodiment of an inanimate object and the strain of the transposition work to be done acutely reminds the audience that a noetical restructuring is required. In the case of dramatic deaths, the two noemata attempt to engage in the regular competitive ambivalent relation basic to theatre but the noematical pairing of the live actor and the corpse is undeniably unambiguous and singular and so the embodiment fails, triggering meta-theatre. From the ambivalent phenomenological stance of the audience-subject, it is not necessary for a staged embodiment to be convincing; it need only be ambiguous in its duality.

In the play-within-a-play situation, ambiguity is re-introduced, where really real deaths meta-theatrically highlight the rule. The characteristic of ambiguity itself becomes the target of meta-theatrically figured play-within deaths. Here, it is possible for the actors also to die alongside their characters because with the insertion of another world-within reality shifts from our world (reality[a]) to the fictional world, which frames the play-within (reality[b]). It is inside the medial frame of reality[b] that the actors die. Freed from the restricting body that protects actor[a], actor[b] is able to counter the controlling rule, concerning the limits of embodiment, by actually dying. The real world (reality[b]) invades the play world (reality[c]). So, ambiguity is again possible in the perception of play-within deaths

12. The Roman gladiatorial contest (which I would not consider to be theatre) is the only exception to the ironclad safety of this conviction. An example of an actual death in a work of art that is frequently mentioned to me in this context is the death of one of the stuntman-charioteers in the famous race scene in *Ben Hur* (1959) that occurred during filming and was left in the final print of the film. Significantly, the intended slant of this story is that hearers are to be shocked not at the accident in filming but at the inclusion of it in the film. This anecdote, however, is not in fact true, and lives in repetition as an urban legend. Urban legends take as their inspiration items of collective societal anxieties. It is interesting to note that this aspect of death in art is worthy of perpetuation as a legend. Likewise, snuff films, although widely believed to exist, have also been proven to be an urban legend. A new and disturbing phenomenon is the stream of videos broadcast of hostages in Iraq being beheaded. These killings remain in the realm of the shockingly actual but the framing medium of recording and transmission creeps uncomfortably towards fictionalizing the representations.

13. Peter Ustinov on playing King Lear (Stratford Festival, Ontario, Canada,

1979) re-counts this anecdote: 'Well eventually you die and you think, "This is the most wonderful moment. I hope the audience doesn't see how relieved I am". And you fall to the floor. From then on, until the end of the play, everybody starts talking terribly slowly in deference to your recent death . . . [and while you're lying there], a terrible itch manifests itself on your left ankle. And you think all sorts of things. It's the worst time of the evening. It's got nothing to do with nerves about lines, it's lying there dead knowing you daren't move because you will destroy the illusion for thousands of people' (Richard Ouzounian, *Stratford Gold: Fifty Years, Fifty Stars, Fifty Conversations*, Toronto: McArthur, 2002, pp. 288–289).

14. Susan Zimmerman reaffirms this assessment in her discussion of the corpse as idol: 'Thus the representation of the corpse on the early modern stage entailed the metatheatrical recognition not only of an illusion, but in effect of a double illusion – an illusion of an illusion. That is, a material, sentient body was supposed to signify an insentient one, severed from 'its real materiality' – a disembodied body . . . As a disembodied body only *in potentia*, the body of the actor was thereby enjoined to represent the unrepresentable on several levels, in what

since they occur at one remove from the absolutely real body of the real-world actor. In the main action of the play-within of Soliman and Perseda contained in *The Spanish Tragedy*, Hieronimo kills Lorenzo, Bel-Imperia kills Balthazar and then herself, leaving three corpses on the stage. When the play-within seems to be at an end, Hieronimo considers the convention, addressing the audience-within:

> Haply you think, but bootless are your thoughts,
> That this is fabulously counterfeit,
> And that we do as all tragedians do:
> To die today, for fashioning our scene,
> The death of Ajax or some Roman peer
> And in a minute starting up again,
> Revive to please tomorrow's audience.
> No, princes: . . . (4.4.76–83)

Boasting of his successful revenge, he holds up the uncertainty of dramatic death, contrasting the actual tragic situation with the audience's expectation of the conventional playing of death – that the actors counterfeit death, rising up to play again tomorrow, leaving only their characters dead. Another case of murder-within occurs in Massinger's *The Roman Actor*. As with Hieronimo's play-within, the inner fiction becomes a vehicle for revenge as the emperor Domitian participates in the play-within and as part of the plot kills the player, Paris. At the moment of his stabbing, Paris exclaims, 'Oh, I am slain in earnest!' (4.2.283). In both plays, the 'earnestness' of the murders is made explicit. The extra-dramatic indicator of certain death at the level of world[b] serves to collapse the inner world, eliminating the tension of denial between reality[b] and reality[c], causing the two corpses to become one.

Ambiguity between phenomena activates doubt on two previously held certainties. The first certainty is that the actor still lives when the character dies. Really real death in the play-within casts this certainty into doubt. The other certainty is that death is absolute. Resurrection in the theatre is the province of the actor who gets up after the death of her character. But the iterated theatrical frame encompassing the play-within puts this power into the hands of any actor-within. As a result, the perceptual tension surrounding play-within deaths extends to the tradition of feigned deaths where the characters are subsequently restored to life (Jasper in *The Knight of the Burning Pestle*, Hero in *Much Ado About Nothing* and of course Juliet). Meta-theatricality in these cases turns on the exposure of the rule by characters dying and then popping up again to display that the rule works. When the characters revive, the fictional world within dissolves to restore the actual world.[15]

In each of the above cases where death is feigned in life, the audience-within is purposely deceived by the performed deaths, but the audience-without is aware of the pretence from the outset. This is not the case with the 'death' of Falstaff at the Battle of Shrewsbury in *1Henry IV*. To avoid an extended battlefield encounter with Douglas, Falstaff falls to the ground, counterfeiting his death. This ruse is successful and Douglas exits, while Falstaff remains an onstage corpse throughout Prince Hal's fight with Percy. It is only after Percy is killed and Hal exits that Falstaff sits up, exposing the fakery of his death:

> (*Falstaff riseth up.*) . . . Counterfeit? I lie, I am no counterfeit. To die is to be a counterfeit, for he is but the counterfeit of a man who hath not the life of a man; but to counterfeit dying, when a man thereby liveth, is to be no counterfeit, but true and perfect image of life indeed. (5.4.114–119)

Playing on the word 'counterfeit' as both a pretence and as a false image, Falstaff sophistically claims here that a corpse is the false image of a live person and that the act of pretending to die, the counterfeiting of a counterfeit, is the true mark of a living man. Significantly, in performance, Falstaff delivers this speech with the corpse of Hotspur (and the body of the living actor playing Hotspur) on the ground beside him. Having played his own play-within, Falstaff worries that Hotspur also is a counterfeit player and may too rise up. And so to be certain of the Percy's death, he stabs him again. The meta-theatrical tension between the corpse that rises up and the one that does not comments tidily on the convention at work. Other characters who are unexpectedly restored to life also address this need for the ambiguous relation of phenomena of fiction and reality. Both *The White Devil* and *The Malcontent* feature characters whom the audience thinks are dead and who rise up in later scenes. These restorative events assure the audience, saying in effect, 'Don't worry. I'm not really dead.' But this message nested inside the fictional play-within performs perceptually in two directions. On the one hand, one aspect of the rule is supported, as an actor who performs his own fictional death does not in fact die. But, on the other hand, the other half of the rule is cast into question as the certainty of the death of the character is undermined, promoting suspicion as to the permanency of fictional death.[16]

Twentieth-century plays engage in more elaborate play with the rules of limitation on embodiment in death. Instead of layering world upon world to establish a repetition of the rule or directly countering the rule, meta-theatrical plays on death adjust the boundaries between the several worlds, creating perceptual ambiguity about the application of the rule. One way this is accomplished is by the merging of two worlds into one. In Genet's *The Balcony*, the character of Arthur performs death in both worlds. He is scheduled to play a corpse in the funeral studio (Scene 7), but before this play-within occurs, he actually gets killed (Scene 5). Irma puts him in the scene regardless: 'He didn't think he'd be acting his role this evening in earnest' (61). Another variation on the relation of the multiple dramatic worlds is the situation where the two worlds run in parallel, with figures from both realms interacting with one another. *Six Characters*

might be called the consummate instance of metatheatricality.' 'Animating matter: the corpse as idol in *The Second Maiden's Tragedy*', *Renaissance Drama*, 31 (2003), pp. 222–223.

15. A famous example occurs at the end of John Dryden's *Tyrannick Love* (1669). When the 'corpse' of Nell Gwyn was to be removed, the actress sat up and chastised the stagehand: 'Hold! Are you mad, you damned, confounded dog?/I am to rise, and speak the epilogue.'

16. The culture of comic books has ingrained this doubt concerning the absolute nature of death in its readers. In a fantastical medium, where superheroes and their nemeses die and are regularly resurrected, often by supernatural means, readers of these series view death with great suspicion. It is an axiom of comic-book culture that a character is not dead until you see the body, and even then death is far from certain. For example, in the comic-book-inspired cult television series, *Buffy the Vampire Slayer* (1996–2003), the title character dies and is brought back to life not once but twice.

in Search of an Author presents a very complex case. When the little girl (The Child) is found drowned and the younger brother (The Boy) shoots himself, the actors are shocked. Some of the actors proclaim that it is real. Others defensively insist that it is a pretence. The Father says 'Pretence? Reality, sir, reality!'. Unconcerned with the pretence or the reality, the manager is merely annoyed that he has wasted so much time on these people (276). The two worlds intersect. The two children, like Arthur, die in both realities. They die as characters in their own play – the play-within. They also die 'for real' since their real-world existence is the same as the play-within. Significantly, they are not actors. They are only characters, real in one world; and so, like actual people who are also real in only one world, they are limited to a single existence and an inflexible death. Likewise in *Rosencrantz and Guildenstern Are Dead*, the two eponymous characters are also only characters. And as such, their deaths are prescribed and unavoidable. Guildenstern lashes out at the Player's casual acceptance of his impending death:

> I'm talking about death – and you've never experienced *that*. And you cannot *act* it. You die a thousand casual deaths – with none of that intensity which squeezes out life . . . and no blood runs cold anywhere. Because even as you die you know that you will come back in a different hat. But no one gets up after *death* – there is no applause – there is only silence and some second-hand clothes, and that's –
>
> death –
>
> (And he pushes the blade in up to the hilt. The Player stands with huge, terrible eyes, clutches at the wound as the blade withdraws: he makes small weeping sounds and falls to his knees, and then right down: . . .) (90)

To the applause of his fellow tragedians, the Player dies a 'theatrical death' inflicted by a knife with a retractable blade. Contrary to the theatrical death of the player, Rosencrantz and Guildenstern disappear when they die, avoiding the perceptual oscillation of the ostended corpse. 'Death is not anything . . . death is not . . . It's the absence of presence, nothing more . . . Now you see me, now you – (*And disappears.*)' (91, 92). One cannot 'be' dead, since, as Falstaff argues, being implies an active portrayal of death. In both *Rosencrantz and Guildenstern* and *Six Characters*, two groups with different existential status confront each other. Death is the ultimate test of who is who.

As a distancing device, meta-theatre reminds the audience of the constructed nature of the theatrical illusion, and so protects the audience from excessive emotional involvement. In this sheltered state, confident that the play is only a play, the audience takes comfort that the staged events are not real. Andrew Gurr, in a recent article 'Metatheatre and the Fear of Playing', identifies among Elizabethan playgoers a 'real fear of illusion, and a revulsion against the deliberate dishonesty it was based on'

Jenn Stephenson

(Gurr, 'Fear': 91). To allay this fear, he suggests that steps were taken by the players to acknowledge the danger of the dramatic illusion by making it explicit to the audience. Meta-theatre is one tool that mitigates the fear of illusion by exposing its existence. Regarding basic embodiment conventions like role-playing and the boy-player of women's roles, commentary on the conventions eliminated fear and disposed of any covert deceit by acknowledging the disguise: 'Tricks with meta-theatricality were an essential outcome of the discomfort writers and their audiences shared, as staging techniques grew more sophisticated, over the dangers that lay in the deceptions of realism' (100, 101). But in the case of really real deaths in the play-within, the effect is just the opposite, because fear is not a factor of the too-real illusion but of the too-real reality. The protection of the illusion of the play as play has been breached by the reality of the play as event. Actors whom the audience assumed to be safe are now dead. Instead of reducing audience concern, the ultimate effect of this invasion is to increase fear, a fear that is the product of doubt. When the death of an actor is raised as no longer an impossibility, the perceptual relation between the fictional- and real-world noemata is destabilized by doubt. Although the death of an actor is an extreme case, fear and doubt experienced by the audience that the play as event will displace the play as play is a constant state. For the audience, the actual death of an actor (by accident or murder) brings the world of the play as event abruptly to our notice. On the list of things that could possibly 'go wrong' during a theatrical event – props that are dropped or broken, actors who miss an entrance or trip on the furniture – the death of an actor is certainly the worst. But as a member of this group of mishaps, it is of a type of events that dispels the safety of the illusion and brings to the fore the hazards of dramatic performance. Stage fright is exactly this same kind of fear but from the actor's point of view. Shakespeare uses this image in Sonnet 23 to describe his speaker overcome by love 'As an unperfect actor on the stage,/ Who with his fear is put besides his part' (1, 2). For the actor, the fear is that his safety inside the fictional world will be abrogated by the flubbing of a line or by an embarrassing costume mishap. It is notable in this context, then, that when an actor loses his character succumbing to uncontrollable giggles, it is sometimes referred to as 'corpsing.' The term is apt since the intrusion of the actual actor aspect is death to the character, and also a kind of death for the afflicted actor.[17] Any 'death' onstage that imperils the relation of the illusion to the framing reality is serious in a medium that depends on the maintenance of a careful ambivalence.

Meta-theatrical events interrupt the careful ambiguity of stage objects to display their innate actual objectivity. Typically, this is achieved through reiteration or a kind of layering process, where the theatre repeats or nests certain devices or conventions and by so doing draws attention to the original. Plays-within-a-play work this way as the complete theatrical enterprise is nested inside itself and so through repetition reminds the audience of the theatrical process with which we are engaged. In fact, the vast

17. My thanks to Peter Thomson and my colleague Judith Fisher for clarifying this colloquial British expression for me and for making the connection between laughter and professional 'death'.

majority of meta-theatrical events operate in this layering mode. However, by examining the causes of the perceived meta-theatrical effect triggered by celebrities, corpses and other similarly peculiar objects, it becomes apparent that there are other, albeit rare, modes by which the theatre generates autopoesis. Through this alternate mode, the apprehending audience-subject is confronted with the (near-) certainty of a single reality. The perceptual fluidity of the dual and ambiguous theatrical perception is replaced by the inflexible single view. It becomes apparent that an absolute reality effect is not the relevant issue in successful audiencing. The audience need not be convinced that the actor is Hamlet or indeed is Hamlet's corpse. The audience need only maintain the oscillating double perspective that the actor is provisionally both himself and Hamlet together. The proximity of the two noemata, either as too close or as too distant, only becomes a factor in unbalancing perception when one noema is replaced by the other, leaving only one. The dynamic interplay of two noemata is essential to theatrical perception. By momentarily arresting the oscillation, meta-theatre points to this ordinary need for duality, presenting in the atypical mode a single impoverished vision. Stopping the perceptual 'play', meta-theatre unplayfully insists on the perception of the real celebrity that is a real celebrity and the real actor who is not dead. The relationship of the paired noemata, which shapes ambivalent theatrical perception by alternating between presence and absence is briefly severed. Significantly, however, the perceptual imbalance caused by a meta-theatrical disruption is temporary, audiences are perceptually quite resilient, and so the normal alternation of the competing noemata of actor and character is soon restored.

Beyond the examples shown here of the disruption of the embodiment-effacement convention by celebrities and corpses, this model of the stubbornly single noema, which activates meta-theatrical reflection may be applied to other aspects of theatrical transposition, notably transpositions of dramatic space and time. In the same way that the actor self 'me' becomes another self 'not me' through the theatrical noesis, the space of 'here' becomes 'not here' and the time of 'now' becomes 'not now.' These are subjective apprehensions and conversions performed by the audience engaged in the act of creating theatre. Clearly, theatrical space and time express the same noematic duality as actor bodies. With this similar perceptual pattern evident, it becomes possible to expand the catalogue of meta-theatrical events into hitherto uncharted territory and to compare meta-theatrical strategies of disruption across usually disparate theatrical elements.

Works cited (directly or indirectly)

Abel, Lionel (1963), *Metatheatre: A New View of Dramatic Form*, New York: Hill and Wang.

Armstrong, Alan (2006), '"What is become of Bushy? Where is Green?": metadramatic reference to doubling actors in *Richard II*', in P. Menzer (ed.), *Inside Shakespeare: Essays on the Blackfriars Stage*, Selinsgrove: Susquehanna University Press, pp. 149–155.

Carlson, Marvin (2003), *The Haunted Stage: The Theatre as Memory Machine*, Ann Arbor: University of Michigan Press.

Casey, Edward S. (1973), 'Translator's foreword' to *The Phenomenology of Aesthetic Experience* by Mikel Dufrenne.

Coleridge, Samuel Taylor (1884), 'Progress of the drama', in W.G.T. Shedd (ed.), *The Complete Works of Samuel Taylor Coleridge*, Vol. 4 ('Lectures upon Shakespeare and other dramatists'), New York: Harper.

Dufrenne, Mikel (1973), *The Phenomenology of the Aesthetic Experience*, trans. Edward S. Casey, Albert A. Anderson, Willis Domingo and Leon Jacobson, Evanston IL: Northwestern University Press.

Fuzier, Jean and Patricia Dorval (1990), 'Forms of metadramatic insertions in renaissance drama 1580–1642', in F. Laroque (ed.), *The Show Within: Dramatic and Other Insets: English Renaissance Drama (1550–1642)*, Montpelier: Paul Valéry University Press, pp. 461–468.

Genet, Jean (1962), *The Balcony* (1956), trans. Bernard Frechtman, London: Faber and Faber.

Gurr, Andrew (1987), *Playgoing in Shakespeare's London*, Cambridge: Cambridge University Press.

———— (2000), 'Metatheatre and the fear of playing' in Robin Headlam Wells, Glenn Burgess and Rowland Wymer (eds.), *Neo-historicism: Studies in Renaissance Literature, History and Politics*, Cambridge: Brewer, pp. 91–110.

Husserl, Edmund (1960), *Cartesian Meditations: An Introduction to Phenomenology*, trans. Dorion Cairns, The Hague: Martinus Nijhoff.

Pirandello, Luigi (1952), *Six Characters in Search of an Author* (1921), in Eric Bentley (ed.), *Naked Masks*, pp. 211–276.

States, Bert O. (1985), *Great Reckonings in Little Rooms: On the Phenomenology of Theatre*, Berkeley: University of California Press.

Stoppard, Tom (1967), *Rosencrantz and Guildenstern are Dead*, London: Faber and Faber.

Suggested citation

Stephenson, J. (2007), 'Singular impressions: Meta-theatre on Renaissance celebrities and corpses', *Studies in Theatre and Performance* 27: 2, pp. 137–153, doi: 10.1386/stap.27.2.137/1

Contributor details

Jenn Stephenson is an Assistant Professor of Drama at Queen's University, Kingston, Ontario. Recent publications include articles in *Theatre Journal* and *Journal of Dramatic Theory and Criticism*. She is at work on a book tentatively titled *Metatheatricality and Shakespeare: The Creation and Collapse of Fictional Worlds*.
E-mail: jenn.stephenson@queensu.ca

Books

Theatre & Performance / Art & Design / Media & Culture / Film Studies

Film, Drama and the Break-Up of Britain

By Steve Blandford / **ISBN 9781841501505**

This book engages with ideas that are highly topical and relevant: nationalism, nationhood and national identity as well as the relationship of these to post-colonialism. However, it does so within the broad field of drama. Examining the debates around the relationship between culture and national identity, the book documents the contributions of actual dramatists and film-makers to the chronicling of an important historical moment.

Breaking down what have been traditional barriers between theatre, film and television studies, the text takes into consideration the very broad range of ways in which the creators of dramatic fictions are telling us stories about ourselves at a time when the idea of being 'British' is increasingly problematic. A very wide range of material is discussed in the book, ranging from box-office hits such as *The Full Monty* to community-based theatre in Scotland and Wales.

£19.95 / $40

intellect. Publishers of original thinking
PO Box 862, Bristol BS99 1DE, UK
orders@intellectbooks.com
www.intellectbooks.com

Studies in Theatre and Performance Volume 27 Number 2 © 2007 Intellect Ltd
Article. English language. doi: 10.1386/stap.27.2.155/1

The One Square Foot project

Dorinda Hultona

Abstract

The One Square Foot *project is a collaborative investigation concerned with the making of 'new work'. It places the 'creative actor', rather than the playwright, at the heart of generating material for performance and addresses the question of dramaturgical structure within interdisciplinary performance as one of its key concerns. It uses the term 'creative actor' to refer to any performer involved in the making of 'new work', regardless of his or her disciplinary background.[1]*

The project locates the 'site' for generating material for performance spatially within a chosen place on planet earth – one square foot in dimension. Each square foot is chosen by the 'creative actors' and artists involved in making the work because of its autobiographical resonance for them, as well as for its historical and/or political associations. For example, one of the square feet chosen as a starting point for making a solo piece of 'new work' marked the very spot in a small alleyway where the 'creative actor' making the performance heard that he would be a father for the first time. In the final performance of this piece, images related to this autobiographical moment were interwoven with others derived from an archival document dating from the Second World War, in which it becomes clear that a father has lost a son.

Keywords

creative actor
Cyprus
site
dramaturgy
reading imagery

One Square Foot performances have taken place both on and around the 'site' of each chosen square foot, and also indoors, in studio and theatre spaces, both in Cyprus and in England; and the question of how performance imagery generated in outdoor spaces, and arguably belonging to, and co-authored by, the spaces *themselves*, might be translated, or transported, into indoor spaces, has been part of our concern.

In total six performances have been created: three in Cyprus and three in England. This article focuses on artistic processes, as well as dramaturgical concerns, related to the three Cypriot performances, and one created in England. It features discussion of a piece, entitled *One Square Foot*, which was selected to represent Cyprus at the 'New Plays from Europe' festival in Wiesbaden, Germany, in June 2006. This piece was developed by Echo-Arts Living Arts Centre, Cyprus, in collaboration with a number of creative artists from both sides of the military border in Cyprus, and from Theatre Alibi, UK.[2] It draws on image and metaphor as well as fragments of autobiographical and historical narrative, and focuses on the old Cyprus Government Railway, which ran across the whole island of Cyprus between 1901 and 1951. Within the walled city of Nicosia, now the last divided city in Europe, it linked the predominantly Turkish and predominantly Greek communities within the district of Kaimakli. As part of their research

1. Different phases of the One Square Foot project have been funded by the Cyprus Theatre Organisation (THOC), the Cyprus Ministry of Education and Culture, the Bi-communal Development Programme, USAID, the United Nations and Echo-Arts. Additionally the UK collaborators, Peter Hulton and myself, have received financial support from the Arts and Humanities Research Council (AHRC), the School of Performance Arts, Exeter, Theatre Alibi and the Mark Ward Fund. The project, as a whole, is co-directed by

Arianna Economou
and myself.
Economou is also
Artistic Director of
Echo-Arts Living
Arts Centre, Cyprus
(www.echo-arts.info),
and I am Artistic
Consultant to
Theatre Alibi, UK
(www.theatrealibi.
co.uk).

2. The core group of
artists involved in
making One Square
Foot comprised:
Arianna Economou
(choreographer and
dancer), Peter Hulton
(video artist and
documenter), Ilker
Kaptanoglu (musician
and composer),
Larkos Larkou (sound
design and
composition), Serhat
Selisik (sculptor and
installation artist),
Horst Weierstall
(installation artist and
documenter) and
myself Dorinda
Hulton (dramaturg
and director).

3. Weierstall's work,
including reference
to Re-turn, is
published in From
Sign to Action
(Cyprus: Moufflon
Publications, 2004).

for the performance, the artists spoke with many Turkish and Greek Cypriots now separated by the buffer zone and living on either side of the dividing line, about their memories of the railway, their childhoods, and living in a mixed community, before the division.

The dramaturgy of One Square Foot continues to evolve and has been shaped by a number of factors, including its tri-lingual, interdisciplinary form, as well as the landscape within which the performance was researched and out of which it sprang. The different strategies shaping the dramaturgy of the piece may be traced back into earlier performances within the research project as a whole. In Cyprus, where the project began in May 2003, the first performances that occurred both on, and around, a square foot, and also in a studio space, were generated by the visual and performance artist Horst Weierstall. Weierstall is a German artist/philosopher who is acutely aware of the physical and political demarcation in Cyprus, and he has considered it in his work for many years.[3]

Weierstall's chosen square foot was visible from his studio window, which overlooks the military border dividing the predominantly Turkish Cypriot community from the predominantly Greek Cypriot community. It was chosen in response to the very recent relaxation of restrictions, making it possible for both Turkish and Greek Cypriots to obtain visas to cross the border, and was situated literally and symbolically in the middle of a tarmac street in the old city of Nicosia, at a junction where road markings suggest the alternative of continuing straight ahead, or following a series of arrows to encircle the block.

Weierstall's One Square Foot solo performances entitled Re-turn occurred in three stages: in the first stage, his chosen square foot in the middle of the street was marked with a white chalk powder from the coastline of Ayios Georgios near Limassol; in the second stage, a sequence of actions suggesting a sense of division in the city, and the breaking down of that division, was performed at the entrance to the artist's studio; and in the third stage, the artist led the audience in a night walk beginning at his chosen square foot in the middle of the street and ending back in his studio [Plate 1].

Weierstall's performances on and around his chosen square foot in the street, and in his studio, were conceived in tandem with each other, and were singly authored. The proximity of the two spaces made it possible to move from square foot to studio within the same time frame; and the events and actions that occurred on and around the square foot located in the middle of the street were essentially different from those performed in the studio. As audience members, however, we were invited conceptually and perceptually as well as literally, physically, to journey, with the 'creative actor', between them.

The question of how performance imagery generated in one place might be translated or transported into another, relatively far away, first presented itself in relation to the One Square Foot solo performance of the

Plate 1: Re-turn, 2003. Studio performance, Horst Weierstall. Marking a sense of division in Cyprus. Echo-Arts.

dancer and choreographer Arianna Economou. This performance was entitled *Seeds*.

Economou's chosen square foot was situated underneath a very old kokkoforous tree just outside the small village of Kalopanayiotis, situated in the centre of Cyprus, in the Troodos mountain range. In that very isolated place, with an 'audience' consisting of just two people – Peter Hulton, acting as documenter, and myself acting as facilitator – Economou shared a number of stories and rituals that grew out of, and were related to, the site itself, as well as her own associations with it.

These autobiographical and historical stories and rituals emerged in conversation with me: Explanations about the ancient kokkoforous tree with its history of protection and concealment during past wars, thinking of the tree as a metaphor for her own family history, seeing the seeds of the tree on the ground, then marking her chosen square foot on the earth with the seeds, feeling the seeds and thinking of them as wishes, explaining that the knotted handkerchiefs in the branches of the tree had been left as

Plate 2: Seeds, 2003. Site performance, Arianna Economou. Wrapped in paper like a wax offering. Echo-Arts.

wishes, prayers by people, remembering her father who had died earlier that year and tying a knot of remembrance for him, telling the story of how her father had fallen from a high wall and fractured his skull, of how she had lain on the wall under the tree and felt that a dragon was flying away with her, then lying on the wall again and being in that moment, moving between past and present in the telling, putting on her father's silk jacket, the one he was married in, and winding silk thread around the poles supporting the branches of the tree, unravelling the thread in the dark interior of the chapel hidden by the tree, winding it around the wrapped body of a wax offering inside the chapel, wrapping her own body in paper, and then the paper being wound and bound by silk thread, connecting her literally and metaphorically to the branches of the tree, and so on [Plate 2].

Economou's performances on and around her square foot underneath the old kokkoforous tree in the mountains lasted for two days. These stories and rituals began initially as a way of introducing us to the place, the dancer not thinking of them as 'performances' but as source material for a piece that she planned to evolve eventually for the studio. It was only gradually over the two-day process that Economou – rather than speaking in the past tense about what *had* happened historically in that place, or about what she had done on previous visits to it, or about what she *might* in the future, in the studio, do – began to recognise that her words and actions, on and around her chosen square foot, were, in the present tense, performative in themselves.

Dorinda Hultona

At the end of the two days in the mountains, we talked together about the possibilities for studio performance in the city and whether such a performance needed to be something completely different in form, albeit perceptually and conceptually connected with the work in the mountains, or whether the basic structure that had evolved on and around the square foot might be looked at in the studio, to sense, in that new place, what had to change or not change, what could change or what we wanted to change.

We talked about the idea of not including any narrative at all in the studio performance: about identifying within the source material the deep dynamics, or structures or phenomena that lived under the ground of the original surface – that were so deep you might not see them immediately – but which were equally strong and urgent, and needed equally to be expressed; and how those manifestations, if not particularised in stories, might be readable by an audience. Economou spoke about little moments, ideas and associations that had emerged on and around her chosen square foot in the mountains, and the possibility of translating and developing these into movement images for performance in the studio: for example, starting with the idea of the tree as a vein of the heart, exploring a way of breathing and moving by feeling the flow of her own blood, and then connecting that feeling with a prayer that she might be able to perceive with her heart; or the idea of knots, knotting a secret, moving in a way suggested by that image; or the idea of darkness and light, revealing, and concealing, revealing some things to the audience, and not others; or the idea of weight, stones, of being burdened.

Mostly, we thought about how Economou, as 'creative actor', might carry a sense of 'site' both with and within her while moving from one place to another – perhaps in the way that nomadic peoples might carry a sense of 'home' with and within them: Representing the physical dimensions of it through material objects, and the perceptual and conceptual ones through image as well as through autobiographical and historical narrative. We therefore recorded ambient sound to carry from the mountains to the city, collected seeds from underneath the tree, water from the sulphur springs nearby and gathered together all the small objects that had been associated with the square foot. We thought of the video documentation as aide-memoire, as well as potentially offering performance imagery in itself; and in our hearts and minds, and specifically in the perceptions and understandings of Economou as 'creative actor', we carried the stories and rituals that had emerged, that had been authored in a way, as much by the square foot and its 'situation' in the mountains as by Economou herself.

We thought about the studio space as well, not just as a physical space but also a 'site' in itself, with all its material qualities and possibilities, as well as all the particular expectations and associations it has accrued to itself. To the basic structure, therefore, we planned to add the technical elements facilitated by the studio as 'site', and also to work within a time frame, as well as at a time of day, convenient to, and expected by, our studio audience – to distil two days of material from the mountains into perhaps two hours for the studio.

We began in the studio by trying to remember and re-create Economou's performances on and around the square foot in the mountains; and almost immediately a number of questions arose. Firstly, there was the question of narrative with communicative intent and whether Economou, as a contemporary dancer, would aesthetically want to incorporate the organisation of such material within studio performance, and still call it dance. Secondly, although highly trained in the processes of Body Mind Centreing and 'authentic movement', Economou was also *not* trained in re-creating imagery in the way that an actor trained in Stanislavski's methodology might be. There was, therefore, not only the question of the dancer aesthetically *needing* to find each narrative moment fresh and new in performance, but also the corresponding lack of training *needed* to make each moment *seem* new and fresh within an already-found structure. Thirdly there was the question of working with some very private material that had been generated in the mountains and whether it could, or should, be performed, or explicitly spoken about, in the very 'public' space of the studio.

Economou and I discussed what we termed 'inter-active authorship', and eventually we developed a dramaturgical structure for the studio piece choosing to work within a narrative frame – and trying to place within that frame a number of movement sequences derived from the images that the dancer had spoken about. At each stage, Economou re-affirmed the choice that the stories, and fragments of stories, should be incorporated into the studio piece. We then associated the narrative elements in the verbal frame with the past tense, in a way mirroring the process that we had shared in the mountains: Beginning with explanations, saying I did this, I did that, this happened, that happened, showing rather than re-living, not trying to make each moment as 'meaningful' as it had been in the mountains, not pretending it was happening here and now in the studio but acknowledging that it *had* happened in the mountains; and then from that base moving into the present, using dance to explore ideas and images.

That was our intention, but interestingly the hesitancy the dancer had with words as learned script meant that, in the studio performance, narrative elements were equally as new and fresh, or more so, than the carefully structured movement tasks; and the sense of performative action and ritual became equally strong in the studio, perhaps more so: because there were more people, more witnesses there, and also because, in the studio, there was a greater use of symbol and representation: the seeds on the floor, for example, representing the square foot in the mountains, the chairs and railings and audience rostra representing the branches of the tree, a set of steps representing the chapel, and so on.

We also thought about including the private material implicitly, rather than explicitly, within the piece, but interestingly again the dancer insisted, or needed even, to test the private material that had emerged in the mountains, explicitly within the public space of the studio. So then we thought about ways of contextualising that material by also engaging the private thoughts of our audience; and, at the start of the composition, Economou invited each member of the audience to take a seed from the old kokkoforous tree, and to make a wish. This gesture was offered as a way of bringing each person's private hopes and dreams into the public space of the studio, but safely, concealed inside his or her own head. Finally, at the end of the piece, protected by all the stories and images that had preceded that moment, Economou spoke her own most private thoughts and prayers aloud: Wrapped and bound in paper and silk, like an offering herself, standing in the middle of the studio space, just as she had stood in the middle of the space underneath the tree in the mountains.

Perhaps also there was a sense of nostalgia for the square foot in the mountains in our studio performance, an association between the square foot and the 'real': A kind of lost paradise where we felt that we had connected, during that short time, with the earth and the sky, and were able to share our deepest dreams protected by the tree – for that is how it had felt for the dancer and her tiny audience. In a way, once we were in the city, the square foot in the mountains became like a memory, perhaps like a faint echo of the memory that displaced people might have of their homeland: The 'creative actor' no more a nomad, but dispossessed.

In England, where a second phase of the project took place in July 2003, performances both on and around three square feet, and also in a studio space, were generated by three 'creative actors' working in conjunction with a number of creative artists in turn.[4] Performances on and around each square foot were co-authored between each 'creative actor' and each creative artist in turn, with each 'creative actor' essentially proposing the 'content' and each creative artist proposing a number of 'form(s)' within which that content might be expressed. Professor Anderson from the School of Biological Sciences at Exeter University advised us on the literal content of each square foot.

Each square foot also arguably acted as co-author, not only through offering the materiality of its changing presence to the work, but also, through its situation in the landscape, suggesting a series of dramaturgical structures to the evolving pieces.

One of my concerns as director and dramaturge has been to explore ways of sequencing imagery in relation to its perception, or reception, by an audience, rather than in relation to notions of internal logic or any stream of internal associations that a 'creative actor', or artist, might make by himself, or herself. Thus, one of my interests in the One Square Foot project has been to investigate how a sense of internal 'movement' – within the perceptual and conceptual understandings of an audience – might be provoked, allowing audience members space within, and between, performance imagery to make their own connections and associations; and, also, within the structure of a piece as a whole, inviting a series of

4. This phase of the One Square Foot project was conducted as part of Theatre Alibi's Research and Development programme. Each 'creative actor' came from a different disciplinary and aesthetic background: Deirdre Heddon is a researcher into autobiography in performance; Daniel Jamieson is a writer of radio plays and stories for performance; and Jordan Whyte is an actress who also trains and lectures in physical theatre. Each creative artist similarly came from a different disciplinary and aesthetic background: Arianna Economou worked in this phase of the project as a choreographer and director; Horst Weierstall, with John Collingswood, acted as installation artists; Helen Chadwick worked as a composer and Duncan Chave as a sound designer. Nikki Sved is Artistic Director of Theatre Alibi, Exeter, UK, and within the project, Sved acted as Artistic Consultant to the performances created in England. I acted as director and, with each 'creative actor', as dramaturge.

The processes and exercises developed within this phase of the project are published by Arts Archives, Exeter, in the form of a DVD ROM under the title *One Square Foot: Interdisciplinary Performer Training* (www.arts-archives. org).

5. Heddon has discussed the making of this performance in *Walking, Writing and Performance: Autobiographical Texts* by Deirdre Heddon, Carl Lavery and Phil Smith, eds., Roberta Mock, Bristol: Intellect (scheduled for publication in 2007).

shifts towards common understandings and empathetic response, a sense of connection and community in a public space.

My interest, then, has led me towards attention concerning the reading of imagery by an audience as a compositional element, and central to this concern has been the attempt to set up a perceptual and conceptual dialogue with an audience, as well as an attempt to sustain that dialogue.

Within the making of the One Square Foot performances in England, therefore, I continued to explore this question of 'internal' movement shared between 'creative actor' and audience, in tandem with the possibilities of 'external' movement; that is, we attempted to use the journey of the 'creative actor' and audience moving physically through the space on, and around, each square foot, as a dramaturgical structure. In *Thousands of Routes*[5] for example, a One Square Foot performance dramaturgically structured by Deirdre Heddon, a researcher into autobiographical performance, and myself, the 'external' physical journey of performer and audience began at her chosen square foot, underneath a Giant Sequoia tree, in an Exeter garden. We then followed a pathway through some bushes before crossing a low ditch into a field, trailed towards a spinney of small trees, and finally wound back through the bushes to a small tree standing beneath the Giant Sequoia. Onto the basic structure of this physical journey, Heddon and I sequenced a number of fragments from three parallel narratives that she had researched. One of these narratives related to the Cherokee people, who were forced to leave their homes in the east of the United States and to walk to north-eastern Oklahoma, in 1838; the second related to the subsistence crofters in the Scottish Highland clearances, which began in1840; and the third related to Heddon's own journey from her roots as a child in Scotland.

Guided by the *physical situation* of the square foot, a dramaturgical structure, or map, emerged, suggesting also its own kind of grammar and punctuation, changes in direction for example, marking the juxtaposition of one text with another as a new paragraph might; a walk between two resting points becoming the dramatic equivalent of a suspensory pause inviting time to reflect on the last image and to wonder about the next; leaving the spinney feeling like a semi-colon, crossing the ditch like a comma, standing around the little tree at the end of the piece like a dot dot dot. . . .

To an extent also, the landscape travelled through in the physical journey matched, like a faint, sensate echo, the landscapes within the journeys narrated – and the objects and people within the physical space became strange visual metaphors for images in the stories: The white feathers left by birds along the pathway becoming a metaphor for the white roses that sprang up on the Trail of Tears, the white roses themselves in the narrative, being a metaphor for the grief of the Cherokee people; or the children playing football in the field, the red brick houses in the distance, the surprise of seeing them after the darkness of walking through the woodland area, their oddity and unreality in the context of the story we were travelling, these 'real' images in the physical landscape becoming like an ironic, contemporary comment upon the new land of Oklahoma, as the Cherokee people might have seen it.

Within the 'internal' journey of Heddon's piece, the square foot that she had chosen represented a sense of 'home', a beginning; and the movement from that starting point took us, as audience, through a series of connections and contrasts, fragments from different perspectives and facts, from an awareness of the presence of the place itself, to Sequoia a chief of the Cherokee people, to the Cherokees and their long walk on which so many of their people died, to Georgia, to Scotland, a global and historical journey that ended with a sense of being close to home despite the distance travelled. It was this '*internal*' journey, held within a dramaturgical structure suggested by the 'external' physicality of the original site, that we were able to take into the studio, as well as the question, both implicit and explicit within it, of how to stay rooted while still always moving – that question offering itself also as a chance alignment, with our exploration as a whole.

Arguably, the performance made in the Summer of 2005, entitled *One Square Foot*, was collaboratively authored. Within the process of generating material for the performance, the 'creative actors' and artists involved in the project chose two square feet, one on either side of the military border in Cyprus, now separated by a buffer zone. On the Greek Cypriot side the chosen square foot was a dusty patch of earth very close to the military border. Permission was only granted for documentation purposes if the cameras were pointed away from the border, and an armed soldier accompanied us as we worked. On the Turkish Cypriot side, we were not allowed to approach the border at all but instead chose a square foot of earth in an apiary that was as close to the border as we could get, and to the corresponding square foot on the other side.

Two 'site' performances took place in the first two weeks of our research for the project, one on either side of the border. Following the strategy initiated in Weierstall's *Re-turn*, and then developed in Heddon's *Thousands of Routes*, both performances took the form of walks. The first started in a little sitting area, just outside the reconstruction of a small railway station in the Greek Cypriot Kaimakli district of Nicosia, and followed the line of the Old Cyprus Government railway that used to link the two districts of Kaimakli. The second also started in a little sitting area near one of the old railway buildings in the Turkish Cypriot Omorfita/Kucuk Kaimakli district of Nicosia, and again we followed the path of the railway that used to link one district of Kaimakli to the other. During each forty-minute walk, small events and actions took place and stories were told, these actions and stories arising out of the landscape itself and features within it, as well as from chance encounters with people on both sides of the border, all of whom met us with unfailing generosity and grace.

Our first walk ended with a 'marking' of our chosen square foot in the dusty earth near the military border, the materials used for this marking

Plate 3: One Square Foot, 2005. Site performance. Installation. Marking one square foot with two halves of a honeycomb. Serhat Selisik.

representing both an honouring of the dead and a hope for the future: a mirror, water, chalk and blossoms similar to those used as offerings in a wayside shrine. Our second walk also ended with a 'marking' of our chosen square foot near the military border, this time in the apiary, with two halves of a honeycomb lent to us by the bee keeper, these materials representing a promise of re-connection and communication between the two communities [Plate 3].

In the final composition for *One Square Foot*, performed in theatre spaces on either side of the border in Cyprus, and then in Wiesbaden,

Dorinda Hultona

Plate 4: One Square Foot, 2005. Theatre performance. The First Movement: The Railway. Arianna Economou. Remembering the railway. Echo-Arts.

6. Three spoken languages were used in the performance: Greek, Turkish and English, the English language being necessary for communication between the 'creative actors' and artists involved in the project. The Greek and Turkish languages were used in direct address to our audiences, and in Germany we used Greek and Turkish, as well as some English, but with simultaneous translation.

Germany, a third square foot was imagined, metaphorically within the buffer zone itself, a place to which we were not allowed access, and therefore representing an imagined space, and future, between the two communities. The dynamic of the walks shared between audience and creative artists in the site performances, translated itself, within the final composition, into the dynamic of a journey taken together, with the audience and creative artists as travellers, moving towards a place of understanding in which the space between them could be marked by a promise, an intention at least to seek reconciliation.

Six video interviews were conducted with elderly people from both sides of the military border, and their stories and memories were interwoven into the piece. Stories were told about those who had died in both the Turkish and the Greek Cypriot communities. Significantly, the two main 'creative actors' in the piece, Arianna Economou and Ilker Kaptanoglu, were from the Greek Cypriot and the Turkish Cypriot communities respectively, and their autobiographical stories formed one of the main threads in the piece, as did their respective performance practices: dance and music[6] [Plate 4].

The structure, and content, of the piece itself was interwoven with metaphors of connection and communication between the two communities: The old Cyprus Government railway that ran from the west to the east coast of Cyprus, connecting all the towns and villages in between, the sewage pipes that ran alongside the railway line and that still run underneath the

Plate 5: One Square Foot, 2005. Theatre performance. The Sixth Movement: Weaving. Arianna Economou and Ilker Kaptanoglu. Serhat Selisik.

buffer zone connecting the two sides, and the bees that fly on both sides of the buffer zone to collect pollen to make their honey.

The composition of the piece occurred in seven 'movements' and within each of them, except for the final one, each of the seven different performance languages was sequenced with each of the others. Video projection began each sequence and was followed by recorded sound composition and performance installation, which were layered together. Stories were then told and enacted by the two main performers, sometimes interspersed with stories recorded on video. These were followed by extended sequences of live music, dance and video. Finally each 'movement' ended with a repeated action in which the audience saw a woman pulling the threads on a weaving loom across the width of the stage, connecting one side with the other, the loom itself with its seven supports providing a dramaturgical structure and metaphorical shape for the piece. The sculptures were there from the outset: A line of scorched black figures that acted as witnesses to the action [Plate 5].

The sequencing of performance languages into repeated patterns within each 'movement' gave a sense of momentum to a dramaturgical structure that was made up by a weaving together of many different stories and images rather than being one that was driven by a single narrative. This sense of momentum was underscored by two strategies: The gradual introduction of the more emotionally charged images into the piece as it progressed; and also the sense that the overall action of the piece

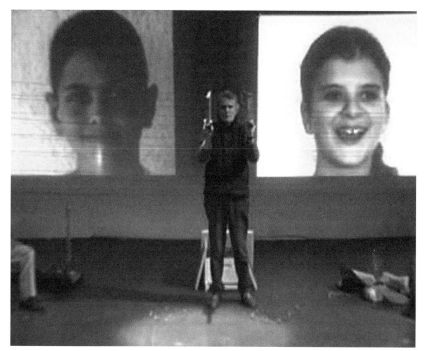

Plate 6: One Square Foot, 2005. Theatre performance. The Seventh Movement: The Future. Horst Weierstall. Marking one square foot with two sides of a honeycomb. Echo-Arts.

(the thing being done by, and within, it) was towards an end point of understanding that was shared between the artists and audience. This sense of shared understanding seemed, and still seems, particularly important in a political situation in which the macro politics of the UN, the EU, the US, Turkey and Greece have dominated the public arena. Our intention was to provide a structure in which our audiences might hear the micro politics of people's experience, hence the subtitle of our piece: *the still small voice of the people.*

The first strategy, referred to above, manifested itself within the titling and ordering of each 'movement', and the second strategy manifested itself in the marking of the metaphorical 'one square foot' in the performance space itself. Thus, in the seventh movement of the piece, entitled *The Future*, the audience sees video images of children from both the Turkish and Greek communities at the same time as hearing a children's choir singing in the Turkish and Greek languages. While this is occurring Horst Weierstall, the performance artist, marks the metaphorical square foot in the performance space with the two sides of the honeycomb, carried into the theatre space from one of our walks. In a way, the composition of *One Square Foot: the still small voice of the people* might be understood as a journey towards this metaphorical marking. [Plate 6].

Suggested citation

Hultona, D. (2007), 'The One Square Foot project', *Studies in Theatre and Performance* 27: 2, pp. 155–168, doi: 10.1386/stap.27.2.155/1

Contributor details

Dorinda Hulton is a part-time Senior Lecturer in Drama and freelance Theatre Director and Dramaturg. Her research, professional practice and teaching focus on 'the creative actor' and the development of processes that facilitate innovative theatre making. Her writings include chapters on Joseph Chaikin for *Twentieth Century Actor Training* (Routledge) and 'the creative actor' in *Theatre Praxis* (Macmillan).

E-mail: D.M.L.Hulton@exeter.ac.uk

Studies in Theatre and Performance Volume 27 Number 2 © 2007 Intellect Ltd
Article. English language. doi: 10.1386/stap.27.2.169/1

Bertolt Brecht's 'Measures against Authority'

Newly translated by Anthony Fothergill

As Herr Keuner, the thinker, lecturing to a hall full of people, was speaking out against authority, he noticed how the people in front of him were shrinking back from him and leaving. He looked round and saw standing behind him – the figure of Authority.

'What were you saying?', Authority asked him.

'I was speaking out in favour of Authority', Herr Keuner answered.

When Herr Keuner had left the hall his students and followers asked him, 'Have you no backbone?'.

He replied, 'I don't have any backbone to be smashed. Above all things I must live longer than Authority.'

And he went on to tell the following story:

One day, in the Time of Illegality, a government agent came to the apartment of Herr Egge, who had learnt to say 'No!'. The agent produced an identity card issued in the name of those who ruled the town and which stated that every home he entered would be his, likewise all the food he desired was his and every person he saw would have to serve him.

The agent sat down on a chair, demanded food, had a wash and then lay down on Herr Egge's bed, and turning his face to the wall before going off to sleep, asked 'Will you serve me?'.

Herr Egge covered him with a blanket, brushed away the flies and guarded him in his sleep. From that day forth he obeyed him for seven long years. But whatever he did for him, one thing he took good care not to do – he didn't say a word. And when, now seven years had passed, the agent had grown fat from so much eating, sleeping and ordering about, he died. Herr Egge wrapped him in the worn-out blanket, dragged him out of the house, cleaned out his room, whitewashed the walls and, breathing out, answered 'No!'.

Translator's note: This – one among many Keuner stories by Brecht – was first published in 1930. The German word *Gewalt* can be translated as 'authority' or as 'force' or 'violence'. Whenever 'authority' is mentioned in this story, these other meanings are also present.

Suggested citation

Fothergill, A. (2007), 'Bertolt Brecht's "Measures against Authority"', *Studies in Theatre and Performance* 27: 2, pp. 169–170, doi: 10.1386/stap.27.2.169/1

Contributor details

Anthony Fothergill teaches English at the University of Exeter. He has also taught at the University of Heidelberg. Other translations include a very early drama by Mozart and 'The Foreign Policy of the Third Reich'. His latest book is *Secret Sharers, Joseph Conrad and his Cultural Reception in Germany'* (Peter Lang Verlag).
E-mail: A.P.Fothergill@exeter.ac.uk

Studies in Theatre and Performance Volume 27 Number 2 © 2007 Intellect Ltd
Interview. English language. doi: 10.1386/stap.27.2.171/7

Theatre and the experience of dispossession

Fateh Azzam in interview with Nicholas Pagan

Abstract

This is the second part of an interview that took place over two days in February
2005 in Fateh Azzam's Cairo home. The first part appeared in STP 27:1, and the
concluding part will appear in STP 27:3.

Fateh Azzam, whose parents were refugees from Haifa, was born in Beirut in 1950. He is a Palestinian with a broad background in theatre, having been a member of a mime performance ensemble that toured the US and Canada in the 1970s and having worked at various times as an actor, director, choreographer and theatre consultant. He has also taught mime, movement and improvisation both in the US and in Ramallah and East Jerusalem. Between 1985 and 1987 he served as director of the Nuzha/El Hakawati Theatre in East Jerusalem. Azzam also became the director of the first Palestinian human rights organization, Al-Haq, based in Ramallah. Since 1987 Azzam has been working primarily in human rights and legal activism. In September 2003 he became the director of the Center for Forced Migration & Refugee Studies at the American University in Cairo.

Azzam's experience as a refugee, an exile and a human rights activist, as well as his extensive immersion in the theatre, have provided him with a unique combination in the domain of artistic expression. In 1991 he turned to writing plays and with Nidal Khatib, Ismael Dabbagh and Abbed Ju'beh co-authored Ansar: A True Story from an Israeli Military Detention Center. The play, which came about mainly as a result of the live testimony of Nidal Khatib, was produced in workshop. Initial performances were so well received that an English version of the play was subsequently taken on tour in the UK, Canada, and the US. Later Azzam went on to write a one act play, Baggage, which was published with Ansar in Short Arabic Plays: An Anthology (2003) edited by Salma Khadra Jayyusi. Baggage was first performed in Arabic in early 2003 at the American University in Cairo as part of the university's annual festival of one-act plays. In October 2003, an English version of the play was performed by Golden State Thread Productions in San Francisco, and on 26–29 April and 13 May 2005 it was performed in the Eastern Mediterranean University Cultural Centre in Famagusta, Northern Cyprus.

In the interview Azzam talks in general terms about Arabic (especially Palestinian) drama, and in some detail about the activities of the El-Hakawati theatre company, before going on to discuss the way in which the two plays – Ansar and Baggage – incorporate experience that is at the same time deeply personal and collective – including the themes of dispossession, occupation, dehumanization and exile.

Pagan: Maybe we can move now to talking about your work as a playwright. English-speaking readers have access to two of your plays: Baggage, which you wrote by yourself and another, Ansar, which was written by you along with some other people. Ansar was first produced for the Palestinian National Theatre in 1991, and you directed the writing and the first performance. Could you tell me something about the process of writing that play?

Azzam: The first thing to notice is that this is actually a true story in the sense that most of the events that take place, most, not all, in the play, Ansar, actually came out of the experience of one of the actors who played in that first production, Nidal Khatib. He was a young aspiring actor. He came to the theatre, and I remember him walking into my office and saying 'I want to act', and I said, 'Well that's nice, do you know how?'. He was a very sweet guy. And then the Intifada started, and he was detained in the Ketziot Detention Centre – administratively, without charge, without trial etc. He came out of prison, and he came to see me (again). He was obviously a different man. So he began to tell me about what had happened to him in prison, some of what the practices were. So that's when I got the idea, and I said, 'Look, this is a theatre piece. And this is something that has to happen.'

So, we started the process to do it, and the agreement and the idea that I had at the time was that this should definitely come out of the experience, but it had to have, of course, theatrical value. Some sense had to be made of that experience of being in that kind of detention centre, in tents, in the middle of the desert, surrounded by barbed wire. So, it was a two-step process. The first step was to get him to tell me stories, long stories, just to get it out of him. And I was taking notes, as he was talking. Not trying to describe the story but taking notes, just thoughts, whatever came to my mind. Then we met several times doing that. Then I asked him actually to write down short paragraphs on each of these, and I pointed out some of the ones that really struck me from all the talking and discussion. So he wrote those, and we gave them each titles, and I put them on index cards. What is this? This is food, torture, dreams – all kinds of things that he remembered from the time when he was there. And I began to put one before the other, and this is all in the imagination, in vague blocks of events or blocks of information. And slowly a shape began to take place. So then, we decided that . . .

Pagan: So up to this point there were only two people involved?

Azzam: Yeah, only two people. Nidal and I. Nidal was telling me his story. He was not involved in any artistic effort yet. Then I started the process of conceptualizing, trying to understand it. Nothing had happened on stage yet; it's all in the air and in the mind. When some preliminary shape began to take place, I figured this has to be. Because a lot of his stories had to do with always one other person. It was never, 'We, all ten of us, went and then we had a meeting, and there were sixteen people in attendance.' It was never about that. It was all about, 'and then this guy came to me and said such and such' or 'we went to this guy and we beat him up, and he came back . . . .'

Pagan: Or he was in solitary confinement?

Azzam: Or he was in solitary confinement. Or, 'I remember one time there was a bird, you know, and this kid tried to catch it. It was so funny.'

Pagan: Or a mouse?

Azzam: Or a mouse. Oh, the mouse I made up actually. So all these scenes were about one person, and his relationship with that one person. So I got the idea that if we take many of these, or many of these individual persons, and have one other actor, so we'd have two people on stage. And that's when we included this other actor and started a process of improvisation: 'OK, take the first card. This is what it is. Tell the story again. Let's talk about it. Let's really talk about what that means.' So the three of us would talk and chat. A little bit later in the process we brought in the fourth guy, the stage manager who could also work with music.

Pagan: So, having heard all these stories, somehow you had to decide which ones to include and which ones not to include.

Azzam: Exactly. And that was basically my decision. How they were included, how they came out as dialogue, how they came out into a partic-ular vignette of storytelling was the work of improvisation. And I'm sitting on the side and the two of them are improvising. They're trying out different types of things – 'Now can you do it with this in mind, for example – he just came to you and told you something that upset you. And now he's coming to you again, pretending like nothing's going on. Can you listen to his story with that first idea in mind, and see what the dialogue brings out?' We kept trying to experiment in that way.

Pagan: Were you taping to have a record of what happened?

Azzam: No we weren't taping, but when we found a piece that we liked, or some dialogue that we liked, we'd say, 'OK. Stop, take a pen and paper and write it down.' And sometimes in writing it down, they would actually develop it a little bit further, because now they were a little bit out of the character and trying to write it down and embellish it a little bit. And sometimes they'd say, 'Oh come one, why'd you do that? Take it out', or, 'Wow, I don't remember that . . . it sort of came out as we were doing it.'

And that's how it went, scene after scene after scene . . . and all the time looking for the thread of meaning throughout the play.

It's all about, when you put a human being . . . you give him a blanket and a change of clothes and put him in a tent with scorpions outside the tent, sometimes often in the tent, and barbed wire, and you're told you're a number, you're not a person anymore, you're a number. And all your basic requirements of life have to be things that you have to work for and that you can lose at any point. It's nothing short of an attempt at de-humanization. It's an effort to make you feel like you are less than a human being. So your resistance has to be, at that level, an insistence on your humanity.

And suddenly I understood what it meant to be writing a letter, and talking about food, and talking about love, and about your sister. 'And don't let so and so sleep in my bed, it's my bed, come on.' It's an insistence on humanity, it's an insistence on love, on things that make life meaningful as a human being, otherwise you are a scorpion like all the other creatures of the desert. Then the meaning of that began to come out. And that meant that we had to review the entire play with that in mind, and keep finding some more . . . it took a long time. Once it started rolling that way, it all made sense. It wrote itself. That's why I say, they were co-authors with me. I can see it, if you will, I can put it together, and I discovered and learned, but I learned from them, I discovered their discoveries. We all wrote it.

Pagan: So was everyone satisfied with the final product?

Azzam: Yeah, everyone was satisfied. The play was in fact a production. It was good. I think it had some problems, from a theatrical point of view. I think its rhythm takes a dip in the middle, it takes it a bit too long to come out of the dip – a kind of broad construction. If I were to rewrite it, I would make some changes, somewhere in the middle . . . you know each play has to have its rhythm. And partly that was the problem, because we were working on each scene, so intensively, that each scene has a very strong and very clear rhythm in itself. But all these scenes together, following the meaning, without paying enough attention to the action, gives a bit of a disturbed rhythm, but that's my opinion.

Pagan: Well, having experience with that process, would you like to do something like that again?

Azzam: I'd love to. To me it's really the height of the creative process. And it's not easy; it's very difficult, because you have to keep reminding yourself about being open, about listening. Creativity is not about quick decisions. You can't be impatient about getting to where you want to go right away: 'Ah ha, Eureka, I've found it!' And once you've said, 'Eureka I've found it', then two days later you might say, 'It doesn't work'.

Pagan: Did you have any experience of this workshop kind of approach to writing plays before Ansar?

Azzam:	I had done this kind of workshop approach to writing original material or to writing theatre in my mime work previously. Then, I was also working on small vignettes, and we'd often work it out as a collective in our group through improvisation; but for Ansar it was a very different kind of process. Working on Ansar, number one – we were starting off with a very real and very painful experience, and we all felt an intense responsibility towards it. And number two – we felt we really had a very strong message that had to come out. That was fantastic, but it also meant that the pressure was on. With mime and improvisation . . . a lot of it is humorous. It's fun. It's enjoyable. You make people laugh and you make people think, and we did a lot of social political commentary, but we didn't have the same kind of personal investment. The feeling was that Ansar was going to make or break what theatre was all about, and what politics was all about at the same time. We dedicated the play to all the detainees in Ansar 3, the military detention facility. Before the first scheduled performance we did an experimental performance only for detainees who were released from that prison camp because we wanted to be sure that they felt that the play represented their experience and their feelings and their dreams about the place. So in a way that kind of relationship to the people who had experienced that horrible time and the message that has to go to the outside world about what that place was really like, was very powerful.
Pagan:	After that first run-through, what kind of audiences did you have?
Azzam:	After it was performed the first few times in Jerusalem, the play went on a tour inside Israel as well, and it was performed, for example, in Palestinian Arab villages in the Galilee . . . We realized that in moving inside the country, inside Israel, we were taking the play to people who were a bit less connected to the occupation. They're still Palestinians, still Arabs, they follow the news, they know what's going on, they know about the prison camps, but they are not living with people who have just been released from such a prison camp. That's happening in the West Bank in Gaza.

With these performances, the realization dawned that – look, this play is a message for those who have no idea. Because, interestingly, performing for the Palestinian community in the West Bank, the play drew some criticisms from people who did not want the Palestinian experience to be portrayed as one of victim. 'What do you mean there was no resistance in the refugee camp? Where's the resistance? Where are the people who are fighting back? That's not us!' It was that kind of reaction . . . even though Kifah resisted, and he was shot; but they didn't like that ending – they wanted some kind of victory over the oppressor.

People in Galilee didn't feel that. They were amazed at what that camp really meant. And that meant that people in the rest of

	the world had to find out. This is a message. This is a detainee's message to the world, a feeling that we have. Then we had a young British fellow who came forward and said, 'I would be really interested in organizing a tour for this play in UK', so we started organizing a tour there.
Pagan:	In the UK?
Azzam:	In the UK, and then in the US and in Canada. So with Ismail and 'Abed and the stage manager – four people – we went on tour. The set was very simple; it was just two wings that looked like a tent and a bunch of stones on the stage. And of course the dummy that comes down. So it was very easy to travel with. We spent three entire months going from place to place performing this play.
Pagan:	In English?
Azzam:	Yes, and we did a few performances in Arabic where there were Arab communities who wanted to have it in Arabic.
Pagan:	Although this play has been translated and performed in English, non-Arabic speakers would not understand some of the Arabic words, like the title itself, 'Ansar', which, I understand, is not merely the name of a detention centre but has other connotations. Perhaps you could explain a little bit about that?
Azzam:	About the title itself?
Pagan:	Yes. I've seen this word 'Ansar' in the Koran, for example, and apparently it is the name given at one point to poor fugitives, dispossessed of their homes and possessions and at another point to those who lead the way in response to the invitation to faith. The people of Ansar, then, were helpers for the prophet. Generally speaking, would Arabic speakers be aware of these 'religious' associations?
Azzam:	The Ansar were those that supported, went to the aid of the first Muslims, if you will, when they were forced out of Mecca, and incidentally most of them were Jews. Most of the Ansar were Jews and Christians in the city of Yathreb.
Pagan:	Jews and Christians?
Azzam:	A few Christians, mostly Jews. Christians often gave shelter to Mohamed as well. But the first Ansar were known to be Jews in Medina. The first hijra, the first dispossession, if you will, drove the early Muslims, the first Muslims out of Mecca. They all ran and sought shelter in Medina. Now, giving shelter and giving asylum is a long-term tradition in tribal pre-Islamic Arabia. And that was also taken in by Islam, becoming a very strong Islamic tradition as well. So they, as the first Muslims were oppressed in Mecca, they took shelter and were given shelter by the Ansar in Medina, most of whom were Jewish tribes.
	In the play, Ansar is the name of the camp, formerly called the Kepziog Military Detention Facility. It is close to the Egyptian

border. But the Israelis had been known to set up camps like this, makeshift detention camps for thousands of people. The first one was in South Lebanon, when they came into South Lebanon in 1982, and they occupied it for a number of years. So they set up that first camp and it was called in that community 'Ansar' because of the area.

Pagan: And then there was Ansar 2 and then Ansar 3 . . .

Azzam: And this was Ansar 3. And essentially all following the same logic: it doesn't matter about facilities, put up some tents, throw up some barbed wire around them, and break in as many of these young activists as you can.

Pagan: One thing that struck me in Ansar was the hunger strikes. I don't know how common hunger strikes were or are in those kinds of facilities. But in Britain we are all familiar with hunger strikes carried out in Northern Ireland, by IRA prisoners, the most famous being Bobby Sands. My question is: does more of the world need to know the names and the stories of similar Palestinian hunger strikers, martyrs?

Azzam: I don't think there have been many that were actually martyred as a direct result of a hunger strike. Bobby Sands is one of very few who got to that point in fact.

Pagan: He was one of a group.

Azzam: Yes, but I mean he died, but how many of the group got to that point and actually died as a result of a hunger strike? There were not too many. There are very few around the world generally. And I don't know of any names of Palestinians who got to that point or to the point of severe suffering as a result of a hunger strike. The idea behind hunger strikes is publicity. You get to draw attention to your plight, to your situation, and it is very commonly employed. Sometimes, perhaps a bit too often, so that it might have lost its efficacy a little bit. In the last three years in Israel there have been a number of hunger strikes. There was one called only recently. It didn't last very long, three days or something. Sometimes they do it for a short time. So it is a very common tool in Palestinian prison culture, if you will to enforce upon the Israeli captor a kind of compromise, in terms of services or in terms of family visits, and all sorts of other reasons.

Pagan: I also was struck in that play by the portrayal of characters as members of a family. For example, the characters Zahran and Kifah talk about getting messages to their families? Zahran at one point in solitary says 'my head, my head, yama, yama, make me a cup of tea'. Now this address to absent family members also occurs in Baggage; for example the traveller recalls the words of his dead father and writes to his mother. It seems that there's a desperate need to contact family members and there is a recollection of family members' words, and this is common perhaps as a

	consolation, perhaps, or a place to turn for guidance. Could we say that one thing that's being represented here is that one of the effects of military occupation and displacement may be to strengthen ties between family members?
Azzam:	I'm not sure. Certainly in Ansar the idea is more – 'I have a root, I come from somewhere. And I want to bring that back to me.' It's not a question of a disruption because of a conflict or argument between family members and then an attempt to bring the family together. It's more a question of 'I am not alone in this world, I cannot accept, here, now, in this place, being alone.' So, in my delirium, I call for yamma; I call for my mother, and I ask her to make me a cup of tea because when I'm home and I'm in trouble, my mother takes care of me, and she brings me a cup of tea, and that's my humanity, that's my connection. I am not alone in this world, and I think this kind of brings that element in.
Pagan:	Consolation?
Azzam:	It's a consolation, and it's also a search for strength. It's a need for consolation and it's a need for strength, looking for strength. I can be stronger when I know that, when this is all over my mother's going to make me a cup of tea; and she's going to tell me everything's ok, and take me in her lap. There's a bit of that. And I think, probably in Baggage, that's the case . . . it's a little bit different in Baggage. I mean that kind of connection is different. The recollection of the father and the father's words is basically 'what am I supposed to do?' It's the question – 'I've got to fix it.' You're almost trapped in that order, you're trapped in that defining moment for your life: 'You broke the radio, you fix it. And you're going to be in the doghouse until you fix it. You're not going to come clear unless that radio is fixed.' It's that that defines your identity or defines your formation; it forms you. So it's a recollection of that, telling the people about that. The letter to the mother in both cases is in part a consolation certainly, but in part you can look at it very coldly just simply as a device, to get that internal dialogue going. In Baggage, it's an internal dialogue issue; the issue is not the mother.
Pagan:	What is the character expressing by communicating with the mother?
Azzam:	In which play?
Pagan:	Well, what is the difference?
Azzam:	In Ansar, it's seeking consolation, it's going back to the warmth of humanity and family. I mean that you know that this message is not going to go, but my insistence, my battle against this occupier, against the Israeli. It's to say, 'Damn you, I'm going to send a letter to my mother, I'm going to send it with a bird and this bird is going to take it home. It's going to fly over home. It's going to take it home and say "I'm alive, and I want you, and I am part of you,

and I will not be just simply a scorpion in the desert."' That's really what is brought out in Ansar.

In Baggage, it's a bit more of a device. It's not so important in itself that he's writing to his mother. It's an excuse to tell what's inside of him, about what it's like to be . . . about the confusion in his life, you know. 'I don't want to fight, I want to do something else, I want to study, I want to be a professor. Let somebody else fight' It's all confusion. He doesn't want anything from his mother. Unless you want to say that security of the home is where you can pour your heart out, but that would probably be a side-effect. It wasn't intended in that sense. Honestly, I just looked at that as the device to get the debate, the internal debate going.

Pagan: But the mother seems to know him, to know aspects of his personal life that other people would not know. And, perhaps that means that he can achieve a level of intimacy with her that he couldn't with other people.

Azzam: Yeah, and that would also be very true when we recall the formative experience of dispossession, the escape under gun fire, the death of Abu Ahmad. His [Traveller's] mother is holding him and Abu Ahmad, the neighbour, is holding him, but then the neighbour is gone. She, the mother, was the partner of that experience, so he will always be attached to her; he will always be going to her – because she is part of the experience, and he had had to take care of her. His father obviously was killed somehow. He didn't see it, he didn't know, but he never made it back from the field; we don't hear from him. So there is of course that special relationship, not only in general between the child and the mother, but also as a partner in the dispossession, as a sharer of an experience.

Pagan: Getting back to performance and Ansar, there's a dream sequence involving the death of Zahran's grandmother. A plastic dummy is used in the sequence, representing the grandmother. Zahran is running frantically to and fro, trying to grab hold of the dummy, trying to save the grandmother, and he's being taunted by an Israeli prison guard at the same time. I'm wondering how this works in performance? In the stage directions the scene is described as being acted out in his imagination. How can this be displayed on stage?

Azzam: Well, we used a screen, so actually what you saw is the shadow of dummy being hung, and taken up with the rope by a soldier on the stage. So the rope went up to a pulley, and from a pulley to a dummy behind the backlit screen. In fact the scene, the dream sequence, is almost like shadow-puppet play, but you see the two physical actors in front of the screen and the representation there . . . . This is actually a dream that Nidal had. This is a proper dream about his grandmother being killed by Israeli soldiers, and we struggled over this for quite some time, trying to figure out – why would you have such a seemingly incongruous dream? Why would the Israeli soldier kill your poor grandmother? What did she do? She didn't throw stones. And then we realized that in a situation like Ansar prison camp, and when we finally hit on the actual scene of dehumanization, it began to make perfect sense. Who's the grandmother? She is his [Zahran's] history. She is his connection to the past. She is the one that taught his mother how to eat the food that is his food that he can still taste in his mouth. She is Palestine. She is the past. So then we reconstructed the scene with that in mind. If you look at the dialogue in that scene, the soldier is taunting him and saying, 'no more grandmother, no more Palestine . . . .'

Pagan: Yes, he says, 'No more grandma, no more history, no more singing.'

Azzam: 'No more singing.' Forget everything that was there in the past. You're here now, and your past is beyond reach. Forget it! You're nothing. You're an insect in the desert. You will die here. So that's when the dream which is a real dream that he really did have in the desert, made sense.

Pagan: There's another dream sequence that stands out for me, and again it involves a family member. This time it's the father – or perhaps he hears his father's voice in his imagination? At this point, Zahran is suffering from food poisoning, and he's delirious. He complains, 'I can't see anymore, yaba, how am I going to find my way?' And his father proceeds to tell the story of Abu Yusef and the hyena. Under a spell, Abu Yusef is led by a hyena to the hyena's den. Then, Abu Yusef hits his head, he wakes up, but we are told it's a bit late now – the hyena is already eating him. So, an obvious question: who or what is the hyena?

Azzam: The hyena is despair, basically.

Pagan: The father also says, 'Zahran, don't let the hyena get out.' What does that mean? Don't express the despair?

Azzam: Don't let despair take you over. Don't let fear defeat you.

Pagan: Negativity?

Azzam: Yes.

Pagan: The Israeli oppressor perhaps?

Azzam: Not so much so. It's more the internal struggle. Your fight within yourself. Where do you find your own strength? And the biggest enemy is within, that's really what it came to. Your biggest enemy is your own fear and your own despair and your own sense of defeat. If you are defeated within, you're defeated outside. If you're not defeated within, nobody can defeat you outside, and the actual battle is within you. It's not with the Israeli occupier. He can do what he needs to do. His task is to break your spirit. It's to defeat you. But the real battle is within yourself, not with him.

Pagan:	As it's an internal struggle, the opposite of despair would be hope then.
Azzam:	Yeah. It would be hope and an insistence on your humanity, and the ability to find the strength within yourself to say, 'No, I'm not going to do that, I'm not going to accept that.' That whole dream sequence . . . and again this is another real dream that Nidal had in the prison. He actually dreamt. He didn't actually have food-poisoning or anything like that. We used that as a way into the dream sequence, but he did actually dream about his father. His father is actually blind in real life. I've met him. He's the sweetest man you would ever want to know. They are from a village south of Bethlehem. Nidal actually dreamed that he had become blind like his father, and he panicked.
Pagan:	This was when he was in the prison?
Azzam:	Yep, he woke up in a panic. That's the extent of the dream. But then we brought in the story of the hyena, ourselves, and continued the dream in that fashion. So then the idea becomes – here is Zahran; he is on the edge of despair really, not only because of all that has happened to him but now he's getting food poisoning; and he feels like he's going to die and he begins to be taken over by despair and by fear, and his father comes to him. And the metaphor here is that, 'I'm blind. I don't know what to do. I don't know where to go. I don't know where I can go from here.' And his father who is also blind is telling him – and in the play you can tell that the father is blind – he, the father, says basically, 'What are you afraid of . . . seeing? You don't just see with your eyes. You see with your heart. You see with your sense. You see with your being.' He tells him the story as a metaphor for the battle with your own despair. The hyena comes at you – and this is a real myth in Palestinian folklore – that if you meet a hyena in the woods at night, they have an enchanting thing about the eye, and they grab you with the eye, and once you let yourself be mesmerized by fear of the hyena they can jump you. So that idea of allowing yourself to be mesmerized by fear, makes you incapable of movement. That's your real defeat.
Pagan:	There's another line in the play related to this. Sa'Adeh says, 'Light a match and the hyena will run.' So there is a clear contrast between the light and the darkness then, between the hope and the despair?
Azzam:	There is something you can do about the hyena. It's up to you.
Pagan:	Another powerful scene in the play involves Zahran in solitary confinement, following the death/martydom of his friend Kifah. Although there's an Israeli soldier praying who, we assume, therefore, does not hear what Zahran is saying, and, part of the time, Zahran addresses a mouse, the scene consists essentially of a monologue. I've noticed that the choice of monologue is quite

	common among Palestinian and other Arab playwrights. Can you think of any particular reason for the prevalence of monologue or mono-drama in this particular context?
Azzam:	A very interesting observation. I remember The Pessoptimist was also adapted for the stage as a monologue. The theatre in Jerusalem did do a number of productions that were monologues as well. I've never really thought of it as a phenomenon to be looked at. I don't know.
Pagan:	Well, you were talking a few minutes ago about internal struggle. If the emphasis is on internal struggle, then Hamlet comes to mind, a play full of monologues/soliloquies – there is tremendous internal struggle going on there. So perhaps it fits into this tradition? Of course you also wrote Baggage as a monologue.
Azzam:	Yes, I chose to write Baggage as a monologue because it is to a large extent about an internal struggle one has with oneself and because I wanted to kept the audience's attention focused on the personal struggle of one person/actor.

In general the choice of monologue could be a throw back to the storyteller tradition. The storyteller is by nature a solitary. He might have a drum or might have a piece of music or he might sing the story sometimes, but he is essentially a solo player. The troupe of troubadours is not a common tradition in our history, but the solo storyteller was. So maybe there's kind of a genetic penchant for monologues? I'm not sure.

Pagan:	And it also connects to the name, Al-Hakawati, the story teller.
Azzam:	Yes, the hakawati, the storyteller, singular.
Pagan:	To finish with Ansar, clearly connections can be made between anecdotes, like that of Abu-Yusef and the hyena that we just talked about, and the monologues also which seem to provide more formal factual information. There's one, for example, which includes the story of the fist Arab leader to call for a popular war of liberation relying on what came to be called guerilla tactics. There's another one which draws attention to the Fourth Geneva Convention on the protection of civilians and the universal declaration of human rights. Ansar ends with Zahran insisting that people have to have knowledge of their history, for without that, they have no firm basis on which to construct tomorrow. The important thing then seems to be not to forget history, symbolized by the friend, Kifah, the martyr and the final image of silhouetted barbed wire. So could we say that Ansar's primary purpose is to serve as a history play or to bring history to the people?
Azzam:	I would say yes, but a very particular history and a very individualized personal history that is shared by the collective. In other words, it is not intended to be a history lesson in terms of what we understand as history, but as narrative, as a people's narrative of their experience; an experiential history perhaps. One that hopes

to record how much these detainees suffered and what they had to go through and to fight for. The idea of the joy of finding a small green sprig that had to be planted, because that's life, that's promoting life. When you are reduced in your humanity to that kind of joy, to finding a bird . . . then the battle between the pragmatic 'I want to eat meat' and the esoteric or the spiritual – 'This is a bird, man. Come on.'

This all needs to be recorded for history, and history is not only what is said at the very end about the different narratives. The interesting part about that scene is that they're actually talking at the same time, so you're hearing two narratives at the same time. So you're actually listening to a lot of facts and the idea of giving each other lessons in history and all of that, but the start of these lessons, is part of the insistence on one's own humanity, and one way to insist on your humanity is to bring back the history and to give yourselves tools with which to struggle, and in this case, the only tool is knowledge, and you have to know your history. And you have this guy teaching you about what happened back then and all of that, and then you have this other one who talks about the national law and humanitarian law and the Geneva convention . . . and they actually did have all of these lessons. Half of the young generation, actually more than half, the generation that is about ten years younger than I, or even my generation, learnt Hebrew in prison. They all speak Hebrew, and they all learned it in prison. It's fantastic. So when you say 'prison is a school', it's very true. And it's the idea of educating one another that is the insistence on the recapturing of your humanity and strengthening your self that comes out of the battle against de-humanization.

Pagan:	And this is the important battle – the battle against de-humanization. It's not history per se. It's not learning a language. It's more.
Azzam:	All of them. In the play this is the battle. It's the battle against de-humanization.
Pagan:	A universal phenomenon?
Azzam:	Yep. I think. But the personal is intertwined with the collective, with the political – completely intertwined in the sense that it's very difficult to separate them. Many of the audiences that came didn't like that last part. He's going, turns around, hasn't changed for fifty years, and they are still doing the same thing to us and we have to keep going, because we don't really have a choice. We have to keep going. Those who wanted heroics didn't like it. It's not enough for them, to just keep going.
Pagan:	What do they want?
Azzam:	They want a very optimistic ending. They want victory. They want to . . . for the theatre to give them in their imagination a victory. Because they think by imagining a victory, they can win, they can get the strength back. See what I mean?

Pagan: Yes.

Azzam: As opposed to, if I feel the depth, if I feel the hyena begin to tear at me, it's up to me to do something instead of hoping that somebody else would give me that hope to latch onto.

Acknowledgement

Nicholas Pagan wishes to record his thanks to Murat Bülbülcü.

Interviewer details

Nicholas Pagan teaches literature, theatre and film at Eastern Mediterranean University in Northern Cyrprus. He is currently working on a project entitled 'American Drama: European and Middle Eastern Crosscurrents'.
E-mail: nicolas.pagan@emu.edu.tr

Notes and Queries

Studies in Theatre and Performance Volume 27 Number 2 © 2007 Intellect Ltd
Notes and Queries. English language. doi: 10.1386/stap.27.2.185/3

Beyond the black box

Kathy Smith

Abstract

The second annual TaPRA conference (CSSD September 2006) made space for the exploration of some interesting issues, and offered the opportunity for academics, practitioners and educationalists to come together to review praxis in the context of current debates and ideas. The particular focus for the Scenography and Visual Performance Working Group, this time round, was the status and role of lighting and sound in the construction and de-construction of the scene; and the Working Group responded to this challenge through practice, in an effort to facilitate an environment that – bringing together the semiotic and the scenographic – would support the meaningful exchange of ideas and the location of a shared vocabulary through which they could be explored. The 'potato workshop', in its apparent simplicity, gave rise to a variety of provocations with both theoretical and practical implications. Drawing on the work of Stephen Lacey and Doug Pye (1994), this article considers some possible implications of the TaPRA workshop in terms of the teaching of the theory/practice relation in theatre and performance studies.

Keywords

hearing
light
scenography
semiotics
sound
TaPRA
vision

Performance is understood in a broad sense, and encompasses the totality of means by which meaning is created in theatre. The kind of approach needed to analyse performance – and establish a necessary critical base – recognises that performance has a material existence, is essentially *constructed* and (essentially) pre-planned and the result of a complex series of decisions and choices. We must regard a performance as a *text* which creates a fictional world that represents and interprets the 'real' one, and which can be subjected to rigorous analysis, as any poem, novel or written dramatic text can. Such an approach is also necessarily structural; that is, it is concerned, at least initially, to establish *how* a performance is addressing us, the ways in which the many different kinds of information that even the simplest performance contains are organised and patterned. (Stephen Lacey and Doug Pye 1994)

In order to be perceived as sound, an action must take place in a volume of air and there must be ears to hear the ripples. In order to be perceived as light, an object or substance in space must be illuminated and there must be eyes to see it.

Given these conditions, no object or effect may accurately be described as purely a phenomenon of light or sound. To know patterned energy as either light or sound I must be immersed in a scene – an arrangement of bodies immersed in non-vacuous space (light can travel in a vacuum but I can't live in one). This arrangement and the story of how that arrangement came to be are not only implied by, but are part and parcel of, any perceived sound object or lighting effect. Even if I am blind or deaf, as long as I know that there is no such thing as silence and that people can't see in the dark, sound and light are fundamental to the meaning of every scene and every performed gesture that transpires. (Ross Brown, TaPRA, 2006)

Last September, the Central School of Speech and Drama hosted the second annual TaPRA (Theatre and Performance Research Association) conference, and I found myself, on the first day, sitting in a drama studio – alongside twenty or so other members of the Scenography and Visual Performance Working Group – contemplating a potato (or rather, a number of potatoes), and wondering, as one of a number of 'theorists' among an eclectic group of academics/practitioners, if I might perhaps have been better suited to a less 'practice-based' gathering. As a group, we were struggling to find a common language: One man was wandering around the circle, stamping on bits of potato, experimenting with the comfort (or otherwise) of standing up, sitting down, lying down or returning to his seat; several others were offering what seemed like random suggestions; props were added and taken away; sound effects were added and taken away; and the whole scene looked a little like organised chaos, punctuated by laughter and by silences. Coming from a background informed by semiotics and psychoanalysis, I offered one or two suggestions; but for a while it seemed that there was little to connect the various contributions.

Reflecting on the difficulty, however, it became clear that what we were experiencing at the outset was in fact the central issue, the lack of common language between the disciplines; and that we were – in practice – *doing* what we were seeking to theorise, i.e. finding ways of bridging the gaps between the disciplines in order to find a common language with which to speak about scenography.

In 1994, an article entitled 'Getting Started: An Approach to Relating Practical and Critical Work', authored by Stephen Lacey and Doug Pye, appeared in *Studies in Theatre Production* (subsequently *Studies in Theatre and Performance*). In this article, Lacey and Pye articulate a related gap: That which was perceived as existing between the 'talking' and the 'doing', the critical and the practical; and they explore how best to allow this relationship to influence course structures. The approach they describe was one that had been developed in the course of teaching the three-year B.A. in Film and Drama at Reading, 'essentially a critical course, the main aim of which [was] to increase students' critical understanding of film and drama and to equip them with the appropriate tools of analysis'. They observe that 'it [was] fundamental to the degree as a whole that "creative" practice and "critical" analysis are conceived as mutually supportive activities'; and that '[o]ne of the central objectives . . . [was] the establishment of a common conceptual language that [could] be used in both areas' (Lacey and Pye: 21).

1. Jiri Veltrusky, 1940, cited in Elam (1980):7.

Lacey and Pye describe an underpinning philosophy and outline a series of 'black box' practical exercises by which students come to understand the manner in which 'meaning' is 'encoded' and 'decoded' within a theatre space, and a vocabulary through which this might be articulated.

More than a decade on, these exercises are likely to be very familiar to most lecturers in theatre and performance, and to generations of graduates of courses all over the country. Certainly, at London Metropolitan University, the 'black box module' (as it came to be known by students) formed, for many years, the core first-year introductory course to the B.A. Theatre Studies programme. It was a course that I inherited from my predecessor, and in an updated version, still teach.

'All that is on stage is a sign'[1]

The course is based on an assumption, grounded in Saussurian and Peircian semiotics, and articulated through systems of theatre/performance analysis such as those of Tadeusz Kowzan, Martin Esslin and Patrice Pavis, that – although the manner in which they interact is significant – the signifying elements of a performance can be examined in isolation from each other. Kowzan's early attempts, in the 1960s, to classify the sign-systems of theatre, highlighted the centrality of the actor to the thirteen systems he identified; and Esslin extended these categories to twenty-two, encompassing additional elements such as architecture and publicity. The Pavis Questionnaire (1985), designed for students with no background in semiotics, provided a useful framing device, and also took greater account of the role of the spectator in the construction of 'meaning'. The work of these practitioners, elucidated and developed in such undergraduate texts as *The Semiotics of Theatre and Drama* (Keir Elam 1980), *Theatre as Sign-System: A Semiotics of Text and Performance* (Elaine Aston and George Savona 1991) and *Directing Postmodern Theater: Shaping Significance in Performance* (John Whitmore 1994), provided a generation of students with a fundamental approach to a systematic analysis of performance, both as spectator and as practitioner, and offered a vocabulary which facilitates both.

More recent models of analysis have explored different strategies for categorisation; but in semiotic terms, the assumption remains, that theatre/performance can be de-constructed to reveal a pattern of exclusive elements.

It was, in effect, this assumption that was explored by the workshop at TaPRA earlier this year. Ross Brown observed that 'calls have been made for consideration of sound and light to figure in research into scenography. These have historically been separately departmentalized in theatre practice and separately categorized in design education. This separation is now increasingly held as problematic' (TaPRA 2006); and two research questions/provocations were constructed:

1. In framing, or attempting to derive information from or impart information to a scene, is it even possible to exclude sound and light? Consider a mute, drab object in a conference workshop – say a potato
   - How much of its potato-ness and how much of its congruity or incongruity with this scene is told by sound and light?
   - What is the remainder of its potato-ness and congruity told by?
2. What were the historical reasons for the categorisation and departmentalisation of sound and light in theatre design? Would it be useful – or even possible – to dissolve these categories in the general term of Scenography? (Ross Brown, TaPRA, 2006)

This provocation was the motivation for the workshop which ensued, a workshop at times frustrating, puzzling, entertaining and challenging. The task in hand was to test the research questions; but in doing so, it was also to find an appropriate vocabulary with which to respond.

Articulating potato-ness

For me, the central question had to concern the issue of whether or not this object could be considered totally in isolation. Semiotic theory would suggest that – within certain constraints – it could. But the question of whether or not we could *see* it without light seemed important; as did the question of whether or not we could *recognise* it without a cultural context within which to decode it. And was it *really* surrounded by silence? Or were we just assuming, because we were not consciously making any noise/sound, that there was no sound (and is 'silence' necessarily the same thing as 'no sound')? We were neither in the dark, nor were we in a dead chamber. Therefore, the object – and the way in which we perceived it – was within a context inseparable from light and sound.

Perhaps its description rested on the *impact* of these elements on it: The identity of the object (and the necessity of a level of cultural competence in order to identify it); the appearance of the object (the colour and texture of which might be altered by lighting); the location of the object (again dependent on being able to see it, but also on aural clues).

At this point in my thinking, the group was experimenting with the way in which a potato bounced when thrown at other surfaces – the sound it made, the sound the surface made (was there a difference?). This use of the potato did suggest to me that we were at that point entering a performance paradigm, where signs become transformable, and a potato could 'become' a football, or the head perched on top of a jacket (and here there was some humour among the group in terms of the notion of eyes, and of 'couch potatoes': again an indication of cultural influence on the construction of 'meaning'). There was some discussion on the significance of the object with which the potato was interacting: The difference between

Kathy Smith

bouncing it off the floor, and dropping it into a frying pan full of hot fat. The latter would, of course, have a cultural significance, not to mention clear visual, aural, olfactory and (if it were at that point touched) tactile implications.

The problem with the hypothesis concerning the bouncing potato was, for me, the notion of 'impact', in that it assumed a prioritisation of one element over the other, and that this was not necessarily implicit. The relation itself then became my focus of attention: It was perhaps not the object (the potato) nor the other 'thing' which held a possible answer, but rather the relationship, or space, between the two, and how they came together?

My next question concerned the prioritisation of vision over hearing: It certainly appeared to be that, in order to identify the object, we needed to be able to see it. We might also be able to identify it by being able to touch it (and this might negate the requirement to see it). We did not necessarily need to hear it in order to identify it (and in fact, we would require some kind of intervention – such as the action of throwing it at the floor – in order to generate an indexical sound; and even then, that sound might tell us more about the object it hit); and smelling it might give even less clue as to its identity.

So *how* do we identify this object: What words or descriptions do we use? And what is the relation between the object and the spectator? How do the sensory 'tools' of the spectator interact with the object? What is the nature of the relation? Millie Taylor, in a recently published article, observes that

> Sound is a physical phenomenon in space that does not only enter the ears, but that interacts with the space and communicates about it, creating an atmosphere that is both communicative and corporeal. Through the impact of vibrations on the receiving body, sound is perceived as a gesture or touch that is impossible to avoid (Taylor 2006: 290).

and that

> while bodies can exist separately in space, so that they may or may not interact at will, sound objects existing in the same space cannot avoid interaction. The vibrations of individual sound objects collide and combine to produce complex and infinitely variable sound worlds (Taylor 2006: 293).

She concludes that 'all sound-waves introduce a relationship between sound-object, space and listener' (Taylor 2006: 295).

Ross Brown suggests that 'even if I am blind or deaf, as long as I know that there is no such thing as silence and that people can't see in the dark, sound and light are fundamental to the meaning of every scene and every performed gesture that transpires' (TaPRA 2006), an observation that highlights issues concerning the existence of silence, and the question of necessity of *both* light and sound in the construction of performance.

And/Or?

The existence and nature of silence (in its possible construction as a positive term rather than description of lack, and also as not necessarily a purely acoustic concept, for one can speak of silences in discourse also) is perhaps an issue best debated elsewhere; but the question of the *necessity* of *both* light and sound in the construction of 'meaning' is open to discussion. In theatre/performance, although it would be difficult to conceive of a theatre where signifiers are constituted of purely touch or smell or taste, meaning can be constructed in the absence of either light or sound (and darkness and 'silence' are on occasion used as signifiers in themselves).

'Noise' is, however, ever-present (an observation foregrounded by the John Cage composition, *4'33"*), either as a product of the auditorium or – if the ears are blocked – as the presence of bodily sounds (heartbeat, breathing, digestive sounds, etc.), as is the vision of darkness (for if you close your eyes, what do you 'see'?).

Brown (2005) asserts that the inevitable presence of *theatre-noise* is inextricable from any signal (visual, verbal or gestural). So although 'meaning' can be – and sometimes is – constructed through the use of darkness or silence, what happens during these moments does not seem to be separable from the bodies and objects within the theatre space.

Furthermore, the performance space itself cannot be separated from the spectator: It is in the relationship between these terms that 'meaning' arises. The *relation between* sound- (and, by extension, light) object, space and listener (and, by extension, spectator) must then become the focus of enquiry.

The terms 'spectator' and 'listener' are, however, not unproblematic; and in Brown's view, these categorised terms are in fact redundant. He suggests that seeing actively probes the external, establishing 'thereness', whereas hearing accepts sound waves, which physically enter the body, establishing 'hereness'. Both, he observes, are always in operation (along with the other senses), and it is in this synaesthetic relationship of 'experiencer' to signals within the theatre-noise field that meaning arises.

Revisiting the 'given'

Returning to the black box exercises, then, and the underlying assumption that – although the elements of theatre interact – each of the elements can be examined in isolation, the issues raised by the 'potato workshop' would suggest that it might be useful – once students have understood the basic concept and function of semiotic analysis – to extend the series of exercises to include a re-consideration of this, by problematising the use of sound and light, and the nature of (i) the sound–object/space/listener relation, (ii) the light–object/space/spectator relation and (iii) the sound/light relation. How, then, might this translate to practice?

Beyond the black box?

My suggestion would be to insert an additional exercise or (given the time constraints on completion of the course) a focused discussion, towards the end of the sequence of student-led exercises, where students might be directed to review their completed exercises to that point within the framework of a different set of constraints, where the focus of the enquiry is shifted, from 'encoding' and 'decoding' of 'meaning', to analysis of either the sound–object/space/listener relation, or the light–object/space/spectator relation.

The exercise/discussion might be framed as follows:

- To what extent is sound/light essential to the construction of 'meaning'?
- To what extent can sound/light be excluded from the performance space?
- What is the role of taste/touch/smell in the construction of 'meaning?
- What is the role of the spectator in the construction of 'meaning'?
- To what extent is the sound–object/space/listener relation a necessary given? Can one term exist in the absence of the other(s)?
- To what extent is the relation between light–object/space/listener a necessary given? Can one term exist in the absence of the other(s)?

Time permitting, a practical exercise might involve the interrogation of a previous presentation by the removal of light or sound and an analysis of the effect of this on the light–object/space/spectator or sound–object/space/listener relation. This exercise might be effected by the introduction of an additional constraint, such as the use of *either* light *or* sound, or a requirement to repeat the previous exercise in the absence of light or sound.

If there is insufficient time to actually do the exercise, then a discussion of the possibility and effects of such a modification to the staging would serve to problematise that which was formerly a 'given'.

Summary

TaPRA, as stated in the constitution, 'exists in order to facilitate research through and into theatre and performance. It is based in collegiality with a formal structure that advances informal, productive and dynamic networks' (TaPRA Information 2006). The 2006 TaPRA conference made space for the exploration of some interesting issues, and offered an opportunity for us, as academics, practitioners and educationalists, to review our practices in the context of current debates and ideas. The Terms of Reference of the Scenography and Visual Performance Working Group, 'taking the scenographic as a particular perspective from which to research theatre and performance', delineate the scope of the working group as that which

- Addresses the visual, sonic, and musical, languages of theatre and performance
- Explores the dynamic relationships between these elements in terms of the sensory experience of the audience.

- Considers ways of scoring, documenting, archiving, and analysing scenographic practice.

(Iball and McKinney 2006)

The particular focus for the S & VP Working Group, this time round, was on the status and role of light and sound in the construction and deconstruction of the scene; and the Working Group responded to this challenge through practice, in an effort to facilitate an environment that would support the meaningful exchange of ideas and the location of a shared vocabulary through which they could be explored. The task in hand was to test the research question, but also to find an appropriate vocabulary with which to respond; and the 'potato workshop', in its apparent simplicity, gave rise to a variety of provocations and exchanges with both theoretical and practical implications.

This opening workshop was followed, in the two subsequent sessions, by a series of presentations exploring the relationship between professional practice and research into scenography, and methods of research and dissemination in scenography and visual performance.

In 1994, Lacey and Pye observed that '[o]ne of the central difficulties we face is that, historically speaking, the languages in which critical and practical work are conducted are often different, sometimes radically so' and that '[o]ne of the central objectives of the foundation course, therefore, is the establishment of a common conceptual language that can be utilised in both areas of work' (Lacey and Pye: 21). Revisiting the original article, in the light of the workshop, the ensuing presentations, and the issues raised, serves to confirm the value of the article in terms of its influence on good practice in the teaching and facilitation of the theory/practice relation in theatre and performance studies: years on, this is still a very solid introduction to the field.

Revisiting the article serves, also, to indicate that time, theory and practice do move on; and although things *have* moved on in the intervening years, there is much scope for further work. TaPRA, as context and vehicle for this, is an engaging prospect.

Acknowledgements

The author would like to thank Ross Brown for leading the workshop described in this article, and for subsequent thoughts and suggestions; Dr Helen Iball for comments and observations; and all the members of the S & VP Working Group who took part in the workshop and presentations, for creating the space to play with ideas.

Works cited

Aston, Elaine and George Savona (1991), *Theatre As Sign-System: A Semiotics of Text and Performance*, London: Routledge.

Brown, Ross (2005), 'The theatre soundscape and the end of noise', *Performance Research*, 10:4, pp. 105–119.

Kathy Smith

Brown, Ross (2006), 'Hands-on workshop: Investigating scenography and visual performance', Unpublished.

Esslin, Martin (1988), *The Field of Drama: How the Signs of Drama Create Meaning on Stage & Screen*, London: Methuen.

Elam, Keir (1980), *The Semiotics of Theatre and Drama*, London: Methuen.

Iball, Helen and J. McKinney (2006), 'TaPRA scenography and visual performance working group: terms of reference', Unpublished.

Lacey, Stephen and Doug Pye (1994), 'Getting started: an approach to relating practical and critical work', *Studies in Theatre Production*, 10, Exeter: University of Exeter, pp. 20–30.

Pavis, Patrice (1985), 'Theatre analysis: some questions and a questionnaire', *New Theatre Quarterly*, 1:2, pp. 209–212.

Taylor, Millie (2006), 'Exploring the grain: the sound of the voice in Bruce Nauman's *Raw Materials*', *Studies in Theatre & Performance*, 26:3, pp. 289–296.

Whitmore, Jon (1996), *Directing Postmodern Theater*, University of Michigan Press.

Suggested citation

Smith, K. (2007), 'Beyond the black box', *Studies in Theatre and Performance* 27: 2, pp. 185–193, doi: 10.1386/stap.27.2.185/3

Contributor details

Kathy Smith is a Senior Lecturer in Theatre studies at London Metropolitan University. Her research interests include theories of identity, spectatorship and representation with particular reference to psychoanalysis, feminism, contemporary theatre/performance practices, and the theatres of Samuel Beckett and Rona Munro.
E-mail: k.smith@londonmet.ac.uk

Books

Contemporary Theatre in Education

By Roger Wooster / **ISBN 9781841501703**

Theatre in Education emerged in the mid-sixties as a unique hybrid of performance and child-centred learning. *Contemporary Theatre in Education* charts the creation and adaptation of this 'hybrid' through the changing political, economic and educational environment. It also takes a 'snapshot' of the TIE being created today, considering all the projects being performed in Wales during a single month. The projects are analysed and every TIE director interviewed about the work and the policies of their companies. It becomes very clear that the distinction between TIE and children's theatre is being blurred.

Is it possible for the hybrid to survive? Or have the economics of schools, the post-National Curriculum educational philosophy and the lack of understanding from a new breed of teachers created an environment that has forced a mutation? Perhaps theatre in education has just evolved, but perhaps just forty years after it began it is facing extinction.

£19.95 / $40

intellect. Publishers of original thinking
PO Box 862, Bristol BS99 1DE, UK
orders@intellectbooks.com
www.intellectbooks.com

Studies in Theatre and Performance Volume 27 Number 2 © 2007 Intellect Ltd
Notes and Queries. English language. doi: 10.1386/stap.27.2.195/3

Dear Editors,

Intrigued by the peculiar query from Martin Banham that you included in STP 26.2 (p. 179), I wish to contribute the following. Not an answer to Martin's query, but rather further evidence that the great man is cracking up somewhat. The following is re-constructed from an e-mail exchange between past and present Professors of Drama at Leeds Universty (he and I).

Yours with concern (for myself as much as Prof. Banham),

Steve Bottoms

Dear Martin,

Just wanted to let you know about the roundtable discussion in the Workshop Theatre on Tuesday 10th October (next week), at 5.45 for 6. Discussing 'the multicultural within the local', vis a vis playwriting. (Though I'm told you prefer the misspelling 'playwrighting'?) We have the West Yorkshire Playhouse Literary Manager and two commissioned play-wrights – Aisha Khan and Tajinder Singh – plus my doctoral student Jackie Bolton. Might be of interest, perhaps?

Hope to see you soon,

Steve

Steve – thanks for the info. Re 'playwrighting', yes I'm a pedant! OK, so *Chambers* allows both, but the *OED* doesn't recognise playwriting. Though alarmingly it does offer 'playwrightess' (a female playwright!).

Best,

Martin

Certainly the consensus as I understand it is that 'wright' is the noun, while 'writing' is the verb. Does 'wrighting' exist anywhere else in the language?

Come on, let's have a fight!

Steve

Well, let's take the U.S. for a start. Say Sonia Sanchez? 'This thing called "playwrighting"'(*African American Review*, Spring 2005).

Martin

[Steve does not reply. Martin insists.]

Dear Steve,

Thoughts whilst mowing the lawn.

Thought 1: Why didn't I do this before it started to rain?

Thought 2: Of course, having thrown Sonia Sanchez into the battle (thinking to floor you with one of your own), I remembered the unhelpful Toby Cole, with *Playwrights on* – yes – *Playwriting*. But undeterred . . . I think my preference (to the point of obsession!) for 'playwrighting' (which, of course, my Apple tells me is an incorrect spelling!) is to some small extent a feeling that 'playwriting' is an Americanisation of the word, but much more fundamentally because it relates to your interesting note in the 'Performing Literatures' conference information. As you say, people like myself 'broke away' from literature departments. Most of us were, by origin, from Eng Lit or Classics or Languages, but were enticed by performance (and dissatisfied with simply dealing with the play as text). In the same way as the wheelwright makes something that moves smoothly, and the shipwright something that floats, so the playwright 'makes' something that performs – not just reads. Obviously this is not a matter of dispute, but – for me – the wrought/wright element is a vital recognition of the visual/performative genius of the playwright who makes something that other people must – back to shipwright – sail, or which assumes a horse or an engine to make it roll. The fact that the playwright reaches his/her audience through the skills of others, and not directly, like the novelist or poet, seems to me to make a crucial difference that should be celebrated and marked out. To limit him/her as someone simply into 'writing' is to diminish the craft. I shall now retire to empty the grass cuttings out of my boots.

Best,
Martin

Dear Martin

I disagree with not a jot of what you say about wrights. The question is whether your perversity in resisting the dictates of the spellchecker makes you an iconoclastic non-conformist or just a bit weird. Personally, I've always liked the fact that playwright is the noun and playwriting the verb, because that in itself is a bit perverse and a bit weird, and it speaks to me where I live about the doubleness of the playwright's role as both a writer of text AND as someone who has wrought something 3-D . . . and the fact that I can only even say that in the past imperfect is extremely weird and thus rather satisfying: Why is there no present tense of the verb 'to have wrought'? I don't know: but the fact that there isn't is also why you can't really have playwrighting . . . (What a wonderfully silly thing the English language is!)

Yours pugilistically,
Steve

Dear Steve,

Clearly we're into weapons at dawn. I choose the *OED* which I shall hurl from a discreet distance. I resent your suggestion that I am just a BIT weird. I didn't get to where I am today by being less than entirely so. Sadly, I suspect that neither of us is entirely 'right'.

(Incidentally, your submission to the spell checker is a sad token of our times. In my day we simply cast them.)

To the death,
Martin

But Martin, you haven't addressed the point about 'wrought' only existing as a past-tense verb. If you can find a present tense use of it, then play-wrighting becomes legitimate. If you can't, ha ha!

My question: does a wheelwright wright wheels?
No. He makes wheels.

Does a playwright wright plays?
No. S/he writes them.

Dead yet?
Steve

A wright is a maker, indeed, but it beautifully implies the total CRAFT, so could we settle on playcrafting ?

Staggering somewhat,

M

I've no objection to playcrafting, but that's not the word that people gener-ally use. We're arguing about the spelling of the one people do use. I feel I've got you on the ropes now, but the roper-dope manoeuvre is an old Ali trick and I'm not falling for it just yet.

S

I bounce back off the ropes. Can I plead for consistency? When I wanted to hone my buoyancy I enquired after the course accredited by the Western Australian Department of Education and Training who offered (and still do) a course in Marine Mechanics Shipwrighting. (Only the lack of 'O' level Latin prevented me taking it up.) Wishing to get a better understand-ing of what makes the world go round I recently looked up B. and J. Morrison's seminal work *Wheelwrighting: A Modern Introduction* (2002). Why one world for the shipwright and the wheelwright, and another for the playwright? Perhaps the always authoritative *Cambridge Guide to Theatre* may help us: 'Early records in Britain refer to "devisers", "doers" and "makers" of plays and games. These unnamed creators share with most great dramatists, many of whom were actors, a common interest and involvement in the actual activity of play. A playwright is one who works play. This is both the craft and essence of theatre.' (And I didn't write that, Les Read did.) A playwright is one who works play, thus playwrighting . . . I smugly suck water off my sponge.

M

Ah, but Martin, the *Cambridge Guide* still doesn't actually use the word playwrighting, despite your having edited it! But I will concede that you know how to use Google, and thus I must concede the points on wheel-wrighting and shipwrighting. Ouch, the old left hook and right jab combination – I crash to the canvas. But the bell goes before the count of ten is complete! – because while you have wrought victory in this battle, I suspect you have lost the war. You have yet to succeed at righting the spellcheckers. And I remain unapologetic in my defence of two separate spellings for noun and verb – inconsistency being precisely the appeal . . .

Best,
Steve

Well Steve, maybe a good time to withdraw to our corners and get our seconds to open the whisky. Love all (to mix my sports), as it were.

M

Does anyone else wish to take up cudgels on this one?

Studies in Theatre and Performance Volume 27 Number 2 © 2007 Intellect Ltd
Notes and Queries. English language. doi: 10.1386/stap.27.2.199/3

Research Assessment Exercise

Panel O, Sub-panel 65
Output Type: I (Performance)
Title: My Life
Place of Performance: Various (UK, US, Continental Europe)
Media of Output: Live performance
Start Date: 1968
End Date: ongoing

For some years, I have been engaged in a piece of durational, multi-locational, yet site-specific invisible theatre called *My Life*. In this piece of Practice-as-Research I am drawing on Goffman and Huizinga to explore performance in life and life in performance. This work has been co-funded by Royal Holloway, AHRC, Arts Council, BBC, and donations in kind.

The boundaries of performance are repeatedly questioned by this conceptual enactment, which is rarely acknowledged as a performance by its (tens of thousands of) spectators – or perhaps 'spectactors', since I allow many of them full and intimate access to the minutiae of *My Life*.

In various phases of my performance work I have built on the work of Burden, Pane and others, testing the limits of the body, its ability to metabolise drink and drugs, its capacity for prolonged sexual experiment, notably in the 'occasional performance' series, *Lost Weekends 1993–2007*. In 2002 I underwent a strenuous investigation of the links between will, mortality and performance in my celebrated *Giving Up Smoking* sequence. I played with the tropes of emotional loss and separation for two virtuoso becoming-solo performances (London 2001; 2006). My *Coming Out & Going Back In Again* durational cycle attempts to shake free notions of personal continuity and coherence in sexual identity.

My Life contains an inter-textual series of sub-performances, many of them performed at internationally-recognised venues like the Royal Court and the National Theatre. These merely professional shows are, of course, not themselves practice-as-research, but I graciously make them so by nesting them in the rigorous theoretical structure of *My Life*. A list of these sub-performances is supplied annually to HM Inspector of Taxes, Grayfield House, Edinburgh.

This performance, which draws on the important insights offered by performance studies, is, you will agree, an important contribution to the debate around Practice-as-Research.

Dan Rebellato

Performing Dark Arts:
A Cultural History of Conjuring

By Michael Mangan / **ISBN 9781841501499**

Magic and conjuring inhabit the boundaries and the borderlands of performance. The conjuror's act of bringing the impossible into being and summoning both the grotesque and marvellous challenges spectators' assumptions of reality and fantasy. *Performing Dark Arts* explores the paradox of the conjuror and the broader cultural implications of magic's assault on human perception. Michael Mangan illuminates the history of the conjuring arts and tests the boundaries of theatrical scholarship by analyzing magic acts alongside more conventional dramatic forms. This book aims to illuminate the history of conjuring by examining it in the context of performance studies, and to throw light on aspects of performance studies by testing them against the art of conjuring. The book examines not only the performances of individual magicians from Dedi to David Blaine, but also the cultural contexts in which their performances were received, and the meanings which they have attracted.

£19.95 / $35

intellect. Publishers of original thinking
PO Box 862, Bristol BS99 1DE, UK
orders@intellectbooks.com
www.intellectbooks.com

Reviews

Studies in Theatre and Performance Volume 27 Number 2 © 2007 Intellect Ltd
Reviews. English language. doi: 10.1386/stap.27.2.201/5

Plays for England, John McGrath, selected and introduced by Nadine Holdsworth, (2005)
Exeter: University of Exeter Press, xi + 340 pp. + 16 illus., ISBN 0-85989-718-4 (pbk), £14.99

This collection gathers together a range of John McGrath's plays written and produced over four decades, many of them for performance by the 7:84 (England) theatre company. It includes a foreword by Michael Billington and an extensive introduction by Nadine Holdsworth that explores the seven plays – *They've Got Out* (1961), *Unruly Elements/Plugged In* (1971), *Trees in the Wind* (1971), *Fish in the Sea* (1975), *Rejoice!* (1982) and *Watching for Dolphins* (1992) – while drawing on archival material, including contemporary newspaper reviews and production photographs, in order to elaborate the theatrical and political context of McGrath's work.

What emerges from this splendid volume is a striking sense of McGrath's theatrical versatility and political preoccupations. Yet it is also the stylistic and formal variation of the individual pieces that really distinguishes this collection. *They've Got Out*, for example, is composed as a brittle, quasi-absurdist dialogue between a married couple who engage in waspish verbal combat, while an unspecified crisis unfolds menacingly outside their house (indeed, the skewed housebound introspection of this mordant pair results in one of the most bizarre closing lines in the entire McGrath canon: 'Oo – look, the crazy paving's started to heave'). *Fish in the Sea*, meanwhile, works within more familiar 7:84 territory, engaging naturalistic and epic modes of theatricality in order to, as McGrath puts it in an early stage direction, '[create] a level of communication and contact with the audience over and above the realities of any one character, or group of characters'. *Watching for Dolphins*, one of McGrath's final plays, takes the form of an evocative and elegiac monologue in which Reynalda, a fifty-something radical, looks back unflinchingly on the failures and possibilities of a lifetime's political activism even as she prepares to commodify herself and her home by opening a bed-and-breakfast for globetrotting tourists in a remote enclave of Wales. Early in the monologue, Reynalda pastiches holiday-brochure clichés in order to indict the rapacious heritage industry and, by implication, her own complicity in it:

> oh boyo – here is the nooky nook to ingle in, the olde-worlde oakie-beamies to Tudor under, the kiss-me-quick canopied beds to four-poster in! (*She pauses, then, with some grief*) Oh, oh, oh – what am I doing to myself?

It's this acutely theatrical combination of playfulness, wit and political bite that adds velocity and emotional depth to much of McGrath's dramatic writing. In this and the other plays included here, McGrath explores the provenance of false and revolutionary consciousness, probes the double-edged but seminal legacy of May 1968, illuminates the deleterious impact of commodity culture on individual and collective experience, orchestrates resonant stage images that give expression to the contradictions of capitalism, and – constantly, continuously, cautiously – asserts the value of solidarity as a means of enabling new, more humane, kinds of living. To be sure, McGrath's writing for theatre has offered an evolving response to prevailing political realities, but his work, too, demonstrates an underlying continuity in its assertion of the fortitude, insights and social agency of women.

Undergraduate students tend to encounter McGrath's work through his polemical and theoretical writings on popular theatre, or else through his landmark play for 7:84 (Scotland), *The Cheviot, the Stag and the Black, Black Oil*. This reasonably-priced collection offers scholars, practitioners and a wider readership a much fuller sense of McGrath's accomplishment as a socialist playwright who remained determinedly 'watching for dolphins' throughout difficult, tempestuous times.

Reviewed by Chris Megson, Royal Holloway College, University of London

Theatre, Body and Pleasure, Simon Shepherd, (2006)
London and New York: Routledge, ix + 198 pp.,
ISBN 0-415-25375-6 (pbk), £19.99

Simon Shepherd opens his pivotal text proclaiming that 'theatre is, and has always been, a place which exhibits what a human body is, what it does, what it is capable of' (p. 1). His book is divided into three parts: the relations between body and script, the relation between theatre bodies and time and space, and finally, the body's supposed integrity. Shepherd, with the greatest of ease in textual movement, glides through certain approaches, like phenomenology, to expose 'theatre as a practice in which societies negotiate around bodily value and bodily order' (p. 10).

My only discomfort with this engaging text is when Shepherd writes that 'Acrobats, gymnasts or dancers are celebrated because of what their bodies can do, rather than what messages they carry' (p. 95). This reference to the dancer's body as a simple athletic mechanism is problematic, as dance, both consciously and subconsciously, choreographs and composes the body as message carrier. Dance offers the choreographer, the dancer and the audience opportunities to discover what the human body represents in various societies, what the human body is able to perform – its limits and possibilities, and what conceptions and ideas of the human body need to be negotiated and re-negotiated, much like Shepherd's propositions about theatre and the body.

Shepherd's bibliography includes a variety of influential dance studies researcher/practitioners, such as Ann Cooper Albright, who states in *Choreographing Difference: The Body and Identity in Contemporary Dance* that 'Twenty years ago, the dancing body was seen as a wonderful source of movement possibilities. Today, however, more and more dancers and choreographers are asking that the audience see their bodies as a source of cultural identity – a physical presence that moves with and through its gendered, racial, and social meanings'.[1] Perhaps, my irritation is a result of my understanding of dance as an act of celebration; occurring when a dancer executes a skilled motif, and, in the moment of performance, a leap of faith, as their dancing body flies through the air, creating meaning through the flying. Yet, this act of celebration also materialises when an actor delivers a substantial piece of text that, too, points to bodily rehearsal and risk, demonstrating what the actor's body can do in performance. It recites text, it moves on stage in relation to the text, it is aware of the audience, it notices the happenings both onstage and in the wings and it engages with other actors and props.

This is a minor irritation, as throughout the book Shepherd clearly and persuasively maps out 'close readings' of his chosen texts, such as 'the opening of Act 2 of Pocock's 1813 play *The Miller and his Men*' (p. 152), drawing on contemporary popular performance and media, like in this particular case, *The X Files*. His strategy offers an excellent method in preparing theatrical texts for performance or academic study. And in my case, coming from a different theatrical and cultural background, a most intriguing and inspiring journey through specific theatrical texts of the western tradition, which, due to Shepherd's focus on the body, has resulted in my understanding of similar historical theatrical texts for bodily pleasure. Moreover, it is his method that is most advantageous to students in particular, and many other researcher/practitioners of performance studies. It is a method that is capable of illuminating and inciting negotiation of bodies in all modes of performance.

Reviewed by Sarahleigh Castelyn, Queen Mary University of London

1. Ann Cooper Albright, *Choreographing Difference: The Body and Identity in Contemporary Dance* (1997), Hanover and London: Wesleyan University Press, p. xxvi.

***Theatre and AutoBiography: Writing and Performing Lives in Theory and Practice*, Sherrill Grace and Jerry Wasserman (eds.), (2006)**
Vancouver: Talonbooks, 352 pp. + 33 illus.,
ISBN 0-88922-540-0 (pbk), $24.99

Theatre and AutoBiography takes its place beside a number of recently published edited collections that have focused on the multiple intersections between theatre and auto/biography, including anthologies by Smith and Watson (2002), Miller, Taylor and Carver (2003), and Gale and Gardner (2004). The appearance of these texts is testimony not only to the diversity of practices and theories (and their points of connection) that can be gathered within the loose category 'theatre and auto/biography', but also to the ongoing need for such critical enquiries, as theatre studies begins to catch up with other disciplines.

The structure and content of *Theatre and AutoBiography* reflects its moment of genesis, a workshop held at the University of British Columbia in 2004, attended by a diverse range of participants with a shared interest in AutoBiography. Arranged into four sections, each with a different, broadly thematic focus, the text is multi-vocal, embracing the academic and the practitioner, the critical theorist and the historian, the performer and the playwright (and those who occupy multiple positions). Though this makes for a less obviously coherent collection, it also proposes that there is something to interest most readers here – whether theories of autobiography and performance; specific plays, productions, companies and practitioners or the use and status of autobiographical documents in the production of theatre history. The ground covered in *Theatre and AutoBiography* is extensive.

The geographical point of genesis is also marked in the text; though analyses and accounts of British and Irish performers are included, the vast majority of papers are focused on the work of Canadian-based artists. This might well be one of the strengths of *Theatre and AutoBiography*, serving to differentiate it from other collections, while also bringing to the attention of a wide public numerous performances that might not be internationally recognised, but which – given their political urgency and/or formal experimentation – should be. Being more than familiar with the work of Karen Finley and Orlan (both of whom, incidentally, are discussed in the anthology), it was a real pleasure to be introduced to, or learn more about the work of, Djanet Sears, Linda Griffiths, Joan MacLeod, Guillermo Verdecchia, Sharon Pollock and R.H. Thomson, to name just some.

Given that discussions of theatre and autobiography often employ a cross-disciplinary methodology, applying theories from English and Cultural Studies, it is gratifying that Part 1, explicitly theoretical in its focus, nevertheless underlines the important difference that theatre makes to the practice of Auto/Biography – in particular the presence of the live body in performance. Susan Bennett's contribution, '3-D A/B', *albeit* (usefully) borrowing from Derrida, asks what impact this body has on our spectatorial response to the Auto/Biographical performances that we witness. As she notes, the visceral presence of the body, before us, exists as both a troubling and enabling authenticating archive (that body sometimes literally carrying the marks of a lived life, as in a body that is wounded; or a body as a palimpsest which carries our previous knowledge of it etc.).

Ric Knowles's contribution relatedly draws attention to the potential for live performance to produce a moment of 'phenomenological *frisson*' (p. 56), where the representational is interrupted by the presentational (or the 'real'). Like Bennett, Knowles is interested in the body as a document of cultural memory, and in the resistant performances that such bodies can enact in the face of dominant histories, serving then, not the 'self' of performance, but a community to which the self is historically connected. Given the frequent charge of Auto/Biographical production as symptom of a self-interested, individualised and bourgeois cultural epoch, the reiteration throughout *Theatre and AutoBiography* of the unavoidable connections between self and others (as explored in Joanne Tompkins's chapter) is a welcome intervention.

The focus of Part 2, though containing important individual discussions, including Tompkins's, is somewhat blurred, even if attention has switched from 'body' to 'play'. As in the previous section, many of the contributors engage with the complexities circulating around AutoBiographical production, including the inevitable existence of 'auto' in biographical work. Any approach to the other can only be made through the self. An unexpected, but not unwelcome contribution is Louise Forsyth's document of an early feminist collective autobiographical performance, *La nef des sorciéres* (1976), which, in terms of its radical content, belongs beside the better-known Californian Womanhouse project.

The historical reclamation performed by Forsyth provides a neat segue into Part 3, where 'Theatre and AutoBiography' refers to the auto/biographical documents relating to theatre practitioners – and how these might be best utilised by theatre historians. Maggie B. Gale, for example, proposes that we engage with them much as we would engage with a performance, employing multiple reading strategies that pay attention to 'the event and the context in which that event is embedded professionally, developmentally, aesthetically, technically, and temporally' (p. 193). Throughout the collection, frequent reference is made to autobiographies' relationship to 'truth', to the lived or historical event and its representation.

The final section of *Theatre and AutoBiography* connects the various theoretical and critical enquiries to practitioners' reflections. Answering a series of questions posed by co-editor Jerry Wasserman, ten Canada-based artists offer thoughtful, illuminating and sometimes provocative replies to issues ranging from how they make their work, to the extent to which they consider themselves to be 'within' their work, to their responsibility to the lives and events they are representing. Though no consensus of opinion is offered, the overwhelming impression is that all creative work is, to some degree, autobiographical; that all representation, autobiographical or otherwise, involves a process of invention; that the primary responsibility the artist has is to the work of art and to the job it has to do; and that 'truth' exists on many levels. As Guillermo Verdecchia writes of his work *Fronteras*, 'I distorted, embellished, and edited many (surface) details in order to get at what I held to be the *meaning* behind the truth of an event or moment' (p. 335). In the end, of course, this can only ever be the artist's meaning (hence the auto in bio), but it is the pressing need to tell this meaning, this story, that drives so many to make work from the details of real lives and to employ creative licence in the process.

Reviewed by Dee Heddon, University of Glasgow

Lilian Baylis: A Biography, **Elizabeth Schafer, (2006)**
Hatfield: University of Hertfordshire Press
(with the Society for Theatre Research), 17 illus. + 291 pp.,
ISBN 1-902806-63-8 (hbk), no price given

This book is an outstanding example of the subtle craft of biography.
Elizabeth Schafer has managed to divide her eleven chapters thematically
without losing touch with chronology. That's not only clever, but also
appropriate. It allows for separate and cohesive treatment of the three
strands in Baylis's life as a theatrical entrepreneur – opera, Shakespeare
and dance – alongside the developing story of a sturdily devout and stubbornly self-willed woman, who came from nowhere in particular to establish herself at the cultural centre of inter-war London. Lilian Baylis was as
unlikely, but never as harmful as Margaret Thatcher. In an acutely framed
appendix, Schafer sketches the various 'afterlives' of her subject, from the
hagiography of Sybil and Russell Thorndike (1938), published within
months of Baylis's death, through the various (predominantly male-
authored) belittlings and mockeries of her achievements and style, to the
Woman's Hour celebration (10 February 2006) of the seventy-fifth
anniversary of her reopening of Sadler's Wells. Schafer's account is as far
from hagiography as it is from mockery. As I was reading the book – and I
read it very quickly, because I was gripped by it – I was made constantly
aware of the extent to which the anecdote industry had suckered me in to
a patronising view of the historical Baylis: the woman with an uncouth
voice, a lop-sided face, irritating dogs and not much more cultural awareness than my great-aunt Fanny Snook, whom she oddly resembled. This
was the image favoured by her arch-denigrator St John Ervine (p. 254)
when he complained that, despite her 'small shop-keeper's mind', she had
'succeeded in imposing upon the world a legend of herself as a mixture of
Joan of Arc, Saint Teresa, and Florence Nightingale' (you see what I mean
about Margaret Thatcher). It is not the image that emerges from Schafer's
measured assessments.

   To be sure, Ervine had some grounds for his invention. Baylis spoke
and wrote of her religious visions (pp. 88–92) and took comfort from God's
backing of the Old Vic, and if 'thrift' was her watchword, it was sometimes
elongated into 'parsimoniousness'. The diptych of 'Saint Lilian and
Shylock Baylis', painted by Ervine, has, then, the authority of caricature.
But it is something altogether grander that survives in Schafer's absorbing
biography: a woman who oversaw the virtual creation of *English* opera
and *English* ballet; who maintained low admission prices without subsidy,
at two major theatres – because she cared more about the local popula-
tions of the Waterloo Road and Islington than about the West End swells;
who treasured the memory of her aunt Emma Cons, who supported her
family and some of her (mostly female) friends and who had the courage
to delegate artistic authority to people as waywardly independent as

     STP 27 (2) Reviews © Intellect Ltd 2007

Matheson Lang, Robert Atkins, Charles Corri, Joan Cross, Ninette de Valois and Tyrone Guthrie. A sharper comparison than Thatcher is Joan Littlewood, who also had a bullying tongue and who also 'found it difficult to weather invasions by the West End at the first hint of artistic success' (p. 261), but who eventually found it impossible to survive without subsidy. Baylis would probably have faced the same problem had she been Littlewood's age. Or would she? Schafer's summarising includes a memorable suggestion: 'The success of her theatres was in no small part due to the fact that Baylis became such a consummate, habitual and entertaining beggar' (p. 267). Imagine being confronted by a Baylis clutching the *Big Issue*.

It is to the credit of the University of Hertfordshire Press that this book is so well produced and so pleasant to hold. The proof-reading has been top-class too. St John Ervine makes a fleeting (unindexed) appearance as Irvine (Sir Henry slipping over from the Lyceum), but the only other error I spotted was the reference to Irving's first female manager, Mrs. H.L. Bateman, as 'Batsman' (so indexed, too) – an excusable outburst of Australian triumphalism after the 2006–7 Ashes series, perhaps.
Reviewed by Peter Thomson, University of Exeter

And Then, You Act: Making Art in an Unpredictable World, Anne Bogart, (2007)
London and New York: Routledge, 140 pp.,
ISBN 0-415-41142-4 (pbk), £14.99

Three years ago, I purchased Anne Bogart's *A Director Prepares: Seven Essays on Art and Theatre*. I had worked in a residency with her SITI company in 1998 and was keen to reintroduce myself to her directing approach and hopefully employ exercises from the book in my own practice. The book, however, comprised of seven essays that were more philosophical than practical, and my initial reaction was of disappointment. I was seeking tangible tools culled from her directing process, and instead found her 'waxing poetic' around themes such as memory and eroticism. Months after my first reading, though, I found myself quoting her work and returning to chapters; delving into the deeper insights contained within her philosophy. *A Director Prepares: Seven Essays on Art and Theatre* has since become one of my most cherished books on directing and creating art.

Bogart's newest book is no less profound and makes a fantastic companion piece. *And Then You Act: Making Art in an Unpredictable World* is similarly structured, containing eight essays on theatre and art-making, written in her signature impassioned and personal style. As she leads the reader through her insights on topics of context, articulation, intention, attention, magnetism, attitude, content, and time, she peppers the writing with informed reflections and poignant anecdotes.

What differentiates this book from *A Director Prepares* is that it inspires artists to continue to create despite extreme global, political and economic obstacles. In the introduction, Bogart describes how a post-9/11 context has reframed her perspective and influenced her art. This post-trauma context is interwoven throughout the book and results in discourses that argue the essential purpose and importance of art in a precarious world. And although her viewpoint is derived from an American subjectivity, Bogart is able to simultaneously embrace and critique her country: 'The new global context has not yet altered our lives as much as it needs to. Americans were not ready for catharsis. We have not made the necessary adjustments. But art can help us to do so. And it is not too late' (p. 9).

Bogart's ability to navigate from the personal to the universal aids her arguments by making them accessible to a variety of readers. Throughout the book, she repeatedly reminds us of the power of words, the magic of theatre and the necessity for artistic expression in societies that experience great ills:

> I believe that if you are making art in these difficult times, you are already successful. The act is the point, more so now than ever. To make theatre in our present climate is a utopian act . . . an act of courage and articulation, a positive action in this convoluted world (p. 47).

Although her book does not provide detailed exercises or guided practical examples to art-making, it is, nonetheless, an important resource for any contemporary artist engaged in the act of creation.
Reviewed by Terri Power, University of Exeter